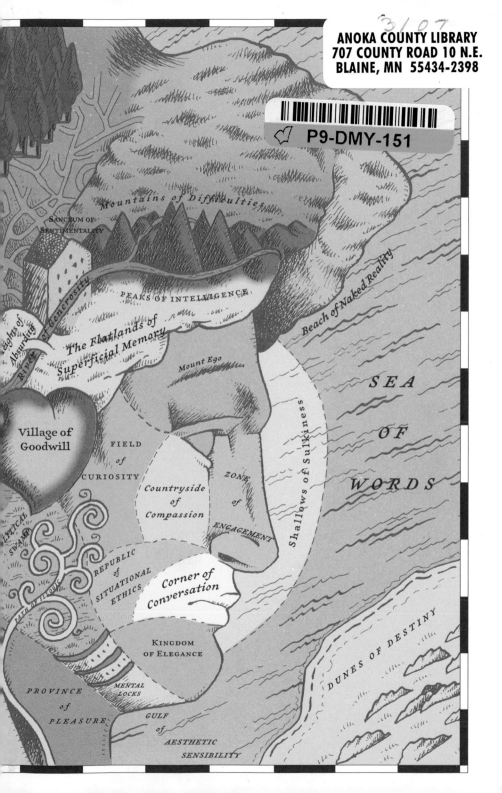

Mountains of Difficulties

SANCTUM OF
SENTIMENTALITY

PEAKS OF INTELLIGENCE

Beach of Naked Reality

Heights of
Absurdity

River of Generosity

The Flatlands of
Superficial Memory

Mount Ego

SEA

OF

Village of
Goodwill

FIELD

of

CURIOSITY

Countryside
of
Compassion

ZONE

of

ENGAGEMENT

Shallows of Sulkiness

WORDS

CRITICAL

SWAMP

PATH OF TRILOGIC

REPUBLIC
of
SITUATIONAL
ETHICS

Corner of
Conversation

KINGDOM
OF ELEGANCE

DUNES OF DESTINY

PROVINCE
of
PLEASURE

MENTAL
LOCKS

GULF
of
AESTHETIC
SENSIBILITY

# La Bella Figura

# Also by Beppe Severgnini

Ciao, America!

# Beppe Severgnini

TRANSLATED BY

GILES WATSON

# La Bella Figura

## A FIELD GUIDE TO
## THE ITALIAN MIND

Broadway Books • New York

Library of Congress Cataloging-in-Publication Data
Severgnini, Beppe.
[Testa degli italiani. English]
La bella figura : a field guide to the Italian mind / Beppe Severgnini ; translated by Giles Watson.— 1st U.S. ed.
p. cm.
1. Italy—Description and travel. 2. Italy—Social life and customs—1945- 3. National characteristics, Italian. I. Title.

DG451.S4813 2006
945.093—dc22
2005058243

ISBN-13: 978-0-7679-1439-0
ISBN-10: 0-7679-1439-2 (alk. paper)

To Indro Montanelli,
as agreed

*At this point, being honest with oneself*

*is the highest form of patriotism.*

LUIGI BARZINI, *The Italians*

# Contents

# La BeLLa Figura

FRIDAY

# Day One: From Malpensa to Milan

**The airport, where we discover that Italians prefer exceptions to rules**

Being Italian is a full-time job. We never forget who we are, and we have fun confusing anyone who is looking on.

Don't trust the quick smiles, bright eyes, and elegance of many Italians. Be wary of everyone's poise. Italy is sexy. It offers instant attention and solace. But don't take Italy at face value. Or, rather, take it at face value if you want to, but don't complain later.

One American traveler wrote, "Italy is the land of human nature." If this is true—and it certainly sounds convincing—exploring Italy is an adventure. You're going to need a map.

So you'll be staying for ten days? Here's the deal: We'll take a

1

look at three locations on each day of your trip. They'll be classics, the sort of places that get talked about a lot, perhaps because they are so little known. We'll start with an airport, since we're here. Then I'll try to explain the rules of the road, the anarchy of the office, why people talk on trains, and the theatrical nature of hotel life. We'll sit in judgment at a restaurant and feel the sensory reassurance of a church. We'll visit Italy's televisual zoo and appreciate how important the beach is. We'll experience the solitude of the soccer stadium, and realize how crowded the bedroom feels. We'll note the vertical fixations of the apartment building, and the transverse democracy of the living room—or, rather, the eat-in kitchen.

Ten days, thirty places. We've got to start somewhere if we want to find our way into the Italian mind.

●  ●  ●

First of all, let's get one thing straight. Your Italy and our Italia are not the same thing. Italy is a soft drug peddled in predictable packages, such as hills in the sunset, olive groves, lemon trees, white wine, and raven-haired girls. Italia, on the other hand, is a maze. It's alluring, but complicated. In Italia, you can go round and round in circles for years. Which of course is great fun.

As they struggle to find a way out, many newcomers fall back on the views of past visitors. People like Goethe, Stendhal, Byron, and Twain always had an opinion about Italians, and couldn't wait to get home and write it down. Those authors are still quoted today, as if nothing had changed. This is not true. Some things have changed in our Italy. The problem is finding out what.

Almost all modern accounts of the country fall into one of two categories: chronicles of a love affair, or diaries of a disappointment. The former have an inferiority complex toward Italian home life, and usually feature one chapter on the importance of the family, and another on the excellence of Italian cooking. The diaries take a supercilious attitude toward Italian public life. Inevitably, there is censure of Italian corruption, and a section on the Mafia.

By and large, the chronicles of love affairs are penned by American women, who display love without interest in their descriptions of a seasonal Eden, where the weather is good and the locals are charming. The diaries of disappointment tend to be produced by British men, who show interest without love. They describe a disturbing country populated by unreliable individuals and governed by a public administration from hell.

Yet Italy is far from hellish. It's got too much style. Neither is it heaven, of course, because it's too unruly. Let's just say that Italy is an offbeat purgatory, full of proud, tormented souls each of whom is convinced he or she has a hotline to the boss. It's the kind of place that can have you fuming and then purring in the space of a hundred meters, or the course of ten minutes. Italy is the only workshop in the world that can turn out both Botticellis and Berlusconis. People who live in Italy say they want to get out, but those who do escape all want to come back.

As you will understand, this is not the sort of country that is easy to explain. Particularly when you pack a few fantasies in your baggage, and Customs lets them through.

* * *

Take this airport, for example. Whoever wrote that airports are nonplaces never visited Milan's Malpensa or Linate, or Rome's Fiumicino. Or, if they did pay a call, they must have been too busy avoiding people shouting into cell phones and not looking where they were going.

An airport in Italy is violently Italian. It's a zoo with air conditioning, where the animals don't bite and only the odd comment is likely to be poisonous. You have to know how to interpret the sounds and signals. Italy is a place where things are always about to happen. Generally, those things are unpredictable. For us, normality is an exception. Do you remember *The Terminal*? If the film had been set in Malpensa Airport, Tom Hanks wouldn't just have fallen in love with Catherine Zeta-Jones. He'd have founded a political party, promoted a referendum, opened a restaurant, and organized a farmers' market.

Look at the childlike joy on the faces of the people as they stroll into the shops. Note how inventive they are at thinking up ways to pass the time. Observe the deference to uniforms (any uniform, from passing pilots to cleaning staff). Authority has been making Italians uneasy for centuries, so we have developed an arsenal of countermeasures, from flattery to indifference, familiarity, complicity, apparent hostility, and feigned admiration. Study the emerging faces as the automatic doors of international arrivals open. They reveal an almost imperceptible hint of relief at getting past Customs. Obviously, almost all the arriving passengers have nothing to hide. It doesn't matter. There was a uniform, and now it's gone.

Note the relief giving way to affection as they retrieve their suitcases from the carousel. At the check-in desk, they weren't sure they would ever see their suitcases again, and did all they could to pass them off as hand luggage. Listen to the couples quarreling, their accusations lent extra ferocity by the embarrassment of performing in public ("Mario! You said *you* had the passports!"). Admire the rituals of the families coming back from holiday. These spoken exchanges—Mom wants to know where their son is; Dad shouts to the son; the son answers Dad; Dad tells Mom, who has disappeared in the meantime—are the same ones that echo in a New York hotel or a street market in London.

Malpensa encapsulates the nation. Only a naïve observer would mistake this for confusion. Actually, it's performance art. It's improvisation by gifted actors. No one believes for one minute he or she is an extra. Everyone's a star, no matter how modest the part. Federico Fellini would have made a good prime minister, if he'd wanted the job. It takes an outstanding director to govern the Italians.

* * *

What else can you find out at an Italian airport? Well, Italians' signature quality—our passion for beauty—is in danger of becoming our number-one defect. All too often, it prevents us from choosing what is good.

Look at the cell-phone displays and the saleswomen perched on their stools. Many of them can't tell a cell phone from a remote control, but all are indisputably attractive. Do you know why the phone companies hire them instead of using skilled staff? Because that's what the public wants. People prefer good looks to good answers.

Think about it. There is a lesson to be learned. We are prepared to give up a lot for the sake of beauty, even when it doesn't come in a miniskirt. "Never judge a book by its cover" sounds like an oversimplification in Italian. We judge books by their covers, politicians by their smiles, professionals by their offices, secretaries by their posture, table lamps by their design, cars by their styling, and people by their title. It's no coincidence that one Italian in four is president of something. Look at the ads here in the airport. They're for cars, bags, and cosmetics. They don't say how good the products are. They tell us how irresistible we'll be if we buy them. As if we Italians needed that kind of reassurance.

* * *

If this passion for beauty stopped at saleswomen, clothes, table lamps, and automobiles, it would be no big deal. Sadly, it spills over into morality and, I repeat, induces us to confuse what is beautiful with what is good. Only in Italian does there exist an expression like *fare bella figura*. Think about that. It's an aesthetic judgment—it means "to make a good figure"—which is not quite the same thing as making "a good impression."

There's an elderly French lady in trouble over there. She's just collected two huge suitcases and can't find a baggage cart. If I went over and offered to help her, she'd probably accept. At that point, something curious would happen. I would split into two. While Beppe was being a Good Samaritan, Severgnini would observe the scene and offer congratulations. Beppe would then acknowledge his own compliment, and retire satisfied.

Ours is a sophisticated exhibitionism that has no need of an audience. Italians are psychologically self-sufficient. What's the problem? Well, we like nice gestures so much we prefer them to good behavior. Gestures gratify, but behaving takes an effort. Still, the sum of ten good deeds does not make a person good, just as ten sins do not necessarily add up to a sinner. Theologians distinguish between *actum* and *habitus:* a single incident is not as serious as a "habit," or "practice."

In other words, if you want to understand Italy, forget the guidebooks. Study theology.

* * *

An aesthetic sense that sweeps ethics aside. A formidable instinct for beauty. That's the first of our weak points. But there are others, for we are also exceptional, intelligent, sociable, flexible, and sensitive. Offsetting these are our good qualities. We are hypercritical, stay-at-homes, so conciliatory and peace-loving we seem cowardly, and so generous we look naïve. Do you see why Italians are so disconcerting? What everyone else thinks of as virtues are our weaknesses, and vice versa.

As I was saying, we are exceptional, and that's not necessarily a good thing. Surprised? Listen to this. Two hours ago, you were on an Alitalia airbus. On other occasions, you've flown American Airlines or British Airways. Did you notice how the cabin staff behaved?

The Italian flight attendant sometimes takes her job title literally—the plane flies, she just attends. But she's always pleasant, elegant, and ladylike, so much so that she can appear intimidating. I remember one flight from Milan to New York. The Alitalia attendant, an attractive brunette from Naples, was strutting up and down like a model on a catwalk thirty thousand feet above the ground. The man sitting next to me glanced at her and asked me, "Do you think I might be able to get another coffee?" "Why ask me? Ask her," I replied, nodding in the direction of the flight attendant. "How can I ask Sophia Loren for a coffee?" he whimpered. He was right. The good-looking attendant was putting on a fashion show in the sky, and no one dared to interrupt.

But then take a British flight attendant. You wouldn't mistake her for a model. She'll have very little makeup, and no jewelry. Often she is robustly built, and until recently would be sporting one of those little round hats that you only see on British cabin staff and New Jersey ice-cream vendors. Her heels are low, and her shoes are "sensible," as they say in New York. Alitalia crews wear emerald green. British Airways has improbable combinations of red, white, and blue, or a mayonnaise-cum-apricot shade that nature felt no need to invent. The British woman is attentive, though. She comes back again and again, smiling all the time. She waits until your mouth is full, swoops on you from behind, and beams "Is everything all right?"

Then something happens. Let's say you spill your coffee on your pants. At that point, the two personalities undergo an abrupt transformation that—you've guessed it—sums up the respective national characters.

The British attendant stiffens. You have deviated from the pattern; you have done something you shouldn't have. All of a sudden, her inner nanny emerges. She doesn't say she's annoyed, but she lets you know.

The attractive Italian also undergoes a change. In an emergency, her detachment disappears. At times of crisis, what emerges is her inner mom, sister, confidante, friend, and lover. She takes off her jacket and actually helps you. Weak at, if not openly irritated by, routine administration, she comes into her own in exceptional circumstances that allow her to bring her personal skills to bear. Where did the ice goddess go? She melted. In her place is a smiling woman who is trying to be helpful.

Do you think some people might be tempted to spill their coffee on purpose the next time they fly Alitalia? Could be. A gorgeous Italian is worth a minor scalding.

•  •  •

OK, let's go. Are you ready for the Italian jungle?

## The highway, or the psychopathology of the stoplight

People say we're intelligent. It's true. The problem is that we want to be intelligent all the time. Foreigners' jaws drop at the incessant brainwaves, the constant flow of imagination, and the alternate bursts of perception and perfectionism. They are stunned by the fireworks display that is the Italian mind. Now, you can astound the English once an hour, the Americans every thirty minutes, and the French on the quarter-hour, but you can't amaze everyone every three minutes—it's upsetting for them. That's why in Italy rules are not obeyed as they are elsewhere. We think it's an insult to our intelligence to comply with a regulation. Obedience is boring. We want to think about it. We want to decide whether a particular law applies to our specific case. In that place, at that time.

Do you see that red light? It looks the same as any other red light anywhere in the world, but it's an Italian invention. It's not an order, as you might naïvely think. Nor is it a warning, as a superficial glance might suggest. It's actually an opportunity to reflect, and that reflection is hardly ever silly. Pointless, perhaps, but not silly.

When many Italians see a stoplight, their brain perceives no prohibition (Red! Stop! Do not pass!). Instead, they see a stimulus. OK, then. What kind of red is it? A pedestrian red? But it's seven in the morning. There are no pedestrians about this early. That means it's a negotiable red; it's a "not-quite-red." So we can go. Or is it a red at an intersection? What kind of intersection? You can see what's coming here, and the road is clear. So it's not a red, it's an "almost red," a "relative red." What do we do? We think about it for a bit, then we go.

And what if it's a red at a dangerous intersection with traffic you can't see arriving at high speed? What kind of question is that? We stop, of course, and wait for the green light. In Florence, where we'll be going, they have an expression: *rosso pieno* (full red). *Rosso* (red) is a bureaucratic formula, and *pieno* (full) is a personal comment.

Note that these decisions are not taken lightly. They are the outcome of a logical process that almost always turns out to be accurate. When the reasoning fails, it's time to call the ambulance.

This is the Italian take on rules of whatever kind, regarding road discipline, the law, taxes, or personal behavior. If it is opportunism, it is an opportunism born of pride, not selfishness. The sculptor Benvenuto Cellini considered himself "above the law" because he was an artist. Most Italians don't go quite that far, but we do grant ourselves the right to interpret it. We don't accept the idea that a ban is a ban, or that a red light is a red light. Our reaction is "Let's talk about it."

\* \* \*

Almost everywhere on the planet, cars stop at pedestrian crossings, most of the time. Where this doesn't happen, either they don't have crossings or they don't have roads. But Italy is a special case. We have roads, which are crowded, and crossings with faded stripes, yet cars rarely stop. They accelerate past, slow down, or swerve. They cut behind, or flit in front of advancing pedestrians, who feel like matadors without a sword to stab the bulls.

Every so often some saint, fool, or foreigner actually stops. Watch what happens. Other drivers behind brake, and make their irritation abundantly clear. They nearly had an accident, and what for? A pedestrian, who might have had the good grace to wait until

the road was clear. The pedestrian assumes a pathetic air of gratitude, forgetting that he or she is exercising a right. Acknowledging
only the concession, the rare privilege, the personal treatment, the
pedestrian crosses and gives thanks. If male and behatted, he might
doff his bonnet, bowing like a medieval peasant.

Thirty years ago, an American journalist pointed out that it's not
chic to be a pedestrian in Italy: it's in bad taste. If there has been any
change, it has been for the worse. In the brutal pecking order of the
highway, Vespas have found a place above pedestrians and below
cars; bicycles are the companions in misfortune of those on foot. Of
course, cars have better brakes than they did thirty years ago. But
there is little consolation in observing how well an ABS works when
it stops a few inches from your ankles. Unless you are one of those
people who come to Italy and find everything picturesque. In that
case, you deserve anything that happens to you. I don't know if
you've noticed, but anything is precisely what does happen on Italy's
roads.

• • •

If human beings express themselves with their vocal cords, tongue,
eyes, and hands, said John Updike, cars use their horns and lights. A
short toot means "Hi!" A longer one means "I hate you!" Flashing
your lights means "After you."

What can we say? Updike has written magisterial novels, but his
automobile semantics is kindergarten stuff. Cast your eye around.
Cars in Italy don't just talk. They make comments, insults, protests,
insinuations, and lectures. They whisper, scream, object, inquire,
whine, and express every nuance of human emotion. And we know
what they're saying.

We compose symphonies on car horns. Nowadays, we use

them less than we used to, but car horns are still expressive, allu-
sive, and occasionally offensive. A short, sharp beep means "I saw
that parking space first!" or "Wake up! The light just changed!" A
longer, disconsolate note wails, "Who left this car in front of my
garage door?" A brief intermittent chirping says, "Here I am," to a
child coming out of school. Some taxi drivers can even toot out
displeasure or solidarity on the horn. They're not disturbing the
peace. It's a sort of superfluous virtuosity, and it's not the only one
in Italy.

And flashing headlights don't mean "After you." To the contrary,
they mean "I'm coming through." Foreigners who fail to understand this message do so at their peril. Flashing headlights in the
passing lane of the *autostrada* mean "Let me by!" And when there
seems to be no reason for the flashing headlights, it means that a police patrol car is just around the corner. This is one of those rare
occasions when Italians, happily hoodwinking the appointed authorities, pull together and show team spirit with total strangers. It's
an uncivil civic spirit that someone ought to study.

*  *  *

Observe the engagingly hysterical traffic, and admire the laid-back
municipal police. Milan's traffic-free zone is busy with authorized
local cars, furious motorists from the hinterland of Lombardy, confused drivers from the rest of Italy, and lost or sneaky Swiss. Just
look at those lines of double-parked vehicles. One is sufficient to
turn an avenue into an alley. Why don't the police do something?
Well, they're tolerant types who have concluded that they can't fine
the entire human race.

They don't make judgments based on unbending rules. They
discuss the motorist's personal choices, displaying a flexibility un-

known to police in other countries. Eavesdrop on one of their conversations. These are summary trials in miniature, with a prosecutor (the police officer), witnesses (another police officer, passersby), a defense lawyer (the wife), mitigating circumstances ("I live right across the street," "I was just going to the pharmacy"), a summing up, and pronouncement of sentence. This weird sort of justice on the hoof—unlike the formal version, which has nine million trials awaiting a verdict and sees eight crimes in ten go unpunished—seems to work.

But tolerance is like wine: a little does you good, too much is harmful. Do you recall those cars hurtling down the fast lane? If you talked to their drivers, you'd discover that the speed limit on the *autostrada*—130 kilometers (about eighty miles) per hour—is not a number, it's an opportunity for debate. It would seem unlikely that the idiot flashing his lights at the car ahead could find any justification for his behavior. But he can. He quotes anthropology, psychology, the principles of kinetics and jurisprudence, imagining favorable interpretations and margins of error, as he places his hopes in the judge's discretion and the mercy of the court.

He ought to be arrested for driving like that, but he deserves a university chair for the way he argues. The listening police officer muses that perhaps he should be tolerant. So he lets the culprit go, thereby punishing the rest of us.

The hotel, where singular people are not content with a double room

D. H. Lawrence wrote in a letter home: "That's why I like living in Italy. People here are so unaware. They feel and want. They don't know." Nonsense. We know very well, and have always known we know. Even when we pretend not to know.

Take this hotel. How is it different from an American motel? In every possible way. An American motel is predictable, replicable, reassuring, rapid, and easy to use. But an Italian hotel, even here in the center of Milan, is unpredictable, surprising, and unrepeatable. It takes time, demands attention, and conceals mysteries. We don't seek reassurance in a hotel; we look for little challenges. We want people to know who we are. We want a good room. We want to hunt for the light switch, styled into invisibility by the decorators.

When a man and a woman check in together at the desk, the reception clerk of a Michigan motel doesn't waste time speculating about their relationship (Friends? Lovers? Colleagues? Father and daughter? A couple breaking up?). It's their business. Here in Milan, the hotel staff are equally professional, the smile is just as ready, and the absence of questions is equally total. But the eyes reveal a not-unpleasant curiosity. It's true that they are nosing into our business. But that means they are thinking about us.

●　●　●

As you can see, this spot is neither picturesque nor charming. It does not deserve any of the adjectives that you foreigners punish us with in your classifications (don't feel guilty—we do the same about you). It's well lit, bustling, and refurbished. It has ninety-four rooms and room service, and is "the only place in Milan where you have high-speed access to Internet and e-mail" (let's hope it isn't, but it's interesting they should say so). In its normality, this hotel explains the workings of Italian hearts and minds, two exotic areas that always come up with new surprises.

The courtesy is not as superficial as it is in other countries, but neither is it as passionate as some non-Italians would like to believe. Let's say that it's a combination of intuition (this is what the customer wants), professionalism (this is what I'm supposed to do), kindness (thou shalt coddle thy neighbor as thyself), shrewdness (a happy customer is a less demanding customer), and good sense (it takes just as much effort to be rude as it does to be polite). All this makes for a warm welcome.

Take note. Lukewarm is the average temperature of Italian social relations. The thermostat is sensitive, and the mechanism kicks in to connect hotel guest and porter, seller and buyer, candidate and voter, inspector and inspected. That's why Italy exports all over the globe superb concierges, military police—the excellent *carabinieri*— exceptional traders, and mediocre scam-merchants.

•  ▪  •

Unlike other people, we're not looking for predictability or uniformity in a hotel. We want to be treated as unique individuals, in a unique place, in unique circumstances. We may be occasional clients of a perfectly ordinary establishment, but we are convinced that in some celestial hotel register—kept by the gods, not the authorities— a trace of our passage will remain.

The Motel Agip chain was Italy's boldest attempt at standardization. It was an interesting cultural experiment with a hint of nationalistic self-sufficiency, but today hotels have taken another direction, which is actually the one they have always followed. Italy's accommodation facilities have to ensure personal treatment and a soupçon of gratification. Run your eye down a list of Milan hotels. You'd think you were in London: Atlantic, Ascot, Bristol, Brun, Continental, Capitol, Carlton, and Carlyle. It's a sort of opening gambit. It tells you to get ready to be astonished.

I'm not the only person to have noticed this. Many of those who have written about Italy—a popular pastime these days—have observed that the country's public life is getting more and more theatrical. Martin J. Gannon, the author of *Understanding Global Cultures*, suggested opera, highlighting four characteristics: pageantry, voice, the externalizaton of emotion, and the interaction of chorus and soloists.

There is pageantry in the uniforms of the porters. You see uniforms in other countries, of course, but Italians wear them with a distinctive *brio*, unlike the coachmen who stand outside some New York hotels (Yogi Bear would wear epaulets with more conviction). The porters may not have braid across their chests, but even in this hotel there is a certain uniformity. Everyone has the same coat and the same badge. They are all reasonably elegant, considering that this is Milan.

Tone of voice is crucial. The receptionist at an Italian hotel knows what we want to keep confidential and what we intend to make public, turning into a secret agent in the first case and a bullhorn in the second. Emotions count. The receptionist offers surprise, a burst of excitement, and the commendable hypocrisy of a tenor-voiced *"Bentornato!"* ("Welcome back!"). The guest is pleased to be recognized, and confident of special treatment. And of course the chorus is important. There is always someone—another porter, a bellhop, or a passing resident—ready to take part in the show, with a gesture, a glance, or a *"Certo, dottore!"* ("Of course, doctor!").

This is usually where Act One, Scene One, finishes. The actors switch off their smiles and disappear behind the scenes. But the performance continues at your room, with the opening of the door, the ritual switching on of the television set, the ceremony of the curtains being drawn back as if for the opening scene, and the illustration of the pillow menu—you can choose from eight types: Ever Comfortable, A Place to Lay Your Head, Supple and Cool, Fit and Ready, Meadow Fresh, The Critical Point, Auping 4, and Auping 1.

Orson Welles used to say that Italy was full of actors—fifty million of them—almost all good. He claimed the few bad ones were on the stage, or the cinema screen. Well, they're certainly not behind the country's reception desks, which are staffed by consummate professionals. Tipping them is not enough. We ought to let them pocket the tourist tax as a supplement to their salary. It would be no more than fair recompense for a classy performance.

* * *

Boarding houses are even more Italian, if that were possible. The name is unique, for a start. *Hotel* and *motel* are international words. *Albergo* is better, but it sounds French. *Pensione* is original, like *bed-and-breakfast*, but the beds are bigger, and the breakfasts smaller.

When I talk about *pensioni,* I don't mean the ones on the tourist-office lists, with their stars and asterisks. A *pensione* (plural: *pensioni*) is any family-run accommodation with a limited number of guests, rooms, and services.

The limited range of services is essential. A TV set is OK, but it shouldn't work properly. The remote might have a dead battery, the colors could be too garish, or Channel 2 might be tuned to the local station. I can accept a phone in the room, but it has to be a model that is no longer available in the shops. I can accept, and indeed applaud, a dining room, but the menu has to be short, with no more than two first courses and three second courses.

A hotel with a long menu, functioning television sets, and a touch-tone phone will never pass muster as a *pensione.* And if it serves breakfast in bed, it should be automatically disqualified. A proper *pensione* is a place that offers a minimum of discomfort, offset by a warm welcome, and the smiles of the dining-room staff, who should be female, not too young, and matronly in appearance. It should be easy to find your way around a *pensione*. There should be a total absence of tunnel-like corridors. There has to be a games room, where younger guests can socialize or squabble over the video games. Otherwise, there should be a *tavernetta* (basement dining area), a working fireplace, or a reading room with piles of last year's magazines.

In recent years, the word *pensione* has come to mean the small hotels in Romagna with names like Miramare (Seaview) that are now full of vacationers from Eastern Europe. *Pensione* owners have been quick to react. Today their establishments are dressed up as something else, as ashamed of their origins as a country girl in the big city. They call themselves "small hotels," "chalets," or *alberghi di charme*. Nothing has changed. What matters is that they are family-run. The owner's delightfully despotic manner has us doing what she wants as she guides, informs, and directs us like foster children assigned by destiny and the local tourist board.

You'll see all this as you travel around. In Italy, we demand from boarding houses what Americans ask of motel chains—reassurance. An Italian *pensione* is one of the cocoons where we can enjoy the illusion of being protected, sheltered, and screened from the perils of the outside world. *Pensione* guests are not fainthearted. They are the cognoscenti of custom, and on holiday look for predictable surprises. They want sunshine after rain, a water ice instead of fruit for dessert, and an interesting-looking diner at the next table.

*Pensioni* are most appreciated at three stages in your life: when you are a child, when you have children, and when you can't stand children any longer. In the intervening period, the bold quarter-century that runs from adolescence to the first severe attack of backache, the charm of the *pensione* is hard to appreciate. When you are young, you tend quite understandably to associate *pensione* with "pensioner," and react accordingly. "Stay in the same place for a fortnight? Never!" But the *pensioni* are in no hurry. They wait until we've been round the world, driven coast to coast across the States, and are fed up with white-water rafting. They know that, sooner or later, we'll be back to see what's for dessert. Perhaps with a non-Italian friend, who will also want a portion.

# Day Two: In Milan

Let's see, now: unaffectedness; self-indulgence; habit; relief; confidence; imagination; recollections; curiosity; lashings of intuition; a pinch of tradition; family, civic, and regional pride; diffidence; conformism; intransigence; realism; ostentation; amusement; and surprising serenity. These are the emotions Italians experience as they prepare to sit at a restaurant table. You should try to experience them, instead of just ordering linguini primavera.

In short, we are consummate professionals of culinary consumption. No one else in Europe eats the way we do. The French know what they are talking about, but they're sliding into affectation. They tend to be fussy, and overdo the sauces. France offers late-Empire cooking, as charming as end-of-summer roses. Italy still has republican vigor grafted onto tradition. For centuries, Italians have sought, and usually found, consolation at the table. We don't *think* that a sauce is tasty, or that an olive oil is good. We know it is. We may lie, of course, out of politeness or calculation. But that, too, is a touch of artistry, if you think about it.

Note that I'm talking about all Italians, not just a hard core of gastronomes. There is a spontaneous gustatory proficiency that cuts across social classes, age groups, income brackets, education, and geographical boundaries. Confident food-related judgment derives from our unaffected approach to the table. If there are any tense faces in this restaurant, it's only because they're worried about the check. But I repeat, people know what to choose and what to avoid. If they choose the wrong starter, it's because they want to be able to complain later. In its own way that, too, is a touch of sophistication.

Statistics confirm this gastronomic pride, which derives more from culinary awareness than from chauvinism. According to a British survey, ninety Italians out of a hundred prefer Italian cooking to other cuisines. No other digestive tracts in Europe are as patriotic. Italian cooking also seems to be the favorite among non-Italians. Some 42 percent of interviewees put *la cucina italiana* in first place, followed by Chinese cooking and French cuisine. Third place might not be good enough for our neighbors over the Alps, but they should take it in a sporting spirit. Losing to the champions is no disgrace.

Italians have the same relationship with food that some Amazonian peoples have with the clouds in the sky—one glance and we know what to expect. Naturally, it has taken time to reach this level. We have endured long intervals of poverty-driven culinary insufficiency. About 1760, the Scottish novelist Tobias G. Smollett wrote, "The house was dismal and dirty beyond all description; the bedcloaths filthy enough to turn the stomach of a muleteer; and the victuals cooked in such a manner, that even a Hottentot could not have beheld them without loathing." Then matters improved, eventually achieving excellence.

The roots of our current international success go back to the late nineteenth century, an age of emigration. In their new countries of residence, Italians opened inns and eateries, offering other Italians the only kind of cooking they knew, the home variety. It was a stroke of genius. The home was a laboratory that had been experimenting for centuries, a place where families blended simplicity with imagination and common sense. Italian cooking during the Renaissance was excellent, but its delights were accessible only to the upper classes. The new Italian cooking that would conquer the world was honest, practical, and working-class. In fact, it was further proof that we Italians are good when we don't try to complicate things.

Of course, Italy, too, is changing, and picking up bad habits. People buy *The Silver Spoon,* or get it as a wedding present, and then leave it on a shelf to gather dust. They'd be better advised to flick through it occasionally, the way Americans do nowadays with the heart-tugging zeal of the recently converted. We eat too much, too often. A century ago, children were toothpick-thin. Seventy years ago, they were slim; forty years ago, they looked well nourished. Today they are overweight. We are increasingly tolerant of precooked and frozen meals. We still haven't descended to American TV dinners, the graveyard of family conversation, but the TV set is on, and the microwave is waiting. Actually, the two electrical appliances look quite similar. And I'm afraid they'll get on increasingly well together in Italy, as elsewhere.

If we want to save the Italian way of eating, we have to focus on pride and distrust, qualities we have in abundance. Some foreign habits have never convinced us, nor will they ever.

Pellegrino Artusi wrote in *La scienza in cucina e l'arte di mangiare bene* (*Science in the Kitchen and the Art of Eating Well*), first published in 1891, the condensed wisdom of Italy on the subject: "On waking in the morning, consider what is most suitable for your stomach. If you feel that it is not entirely free from food, restrict yourself to a cup of black coffee." It was a prophetic condemnation of the English-speaking world's breakfast, which is suitable for facing moors, commutes, or hesitant glances, but not for a June morning in Italy.

● ● ●

We're now between Via Meravigli and Corso Magenta, a land of well-heeled residents and courageous visitors. The road surface is sadistically elegant, for it offers three potentially perilous possibilities: perfidious porphyry, unprincipled paving, and terrible tramlines. It is the ultimate road race for cyclists and motorbikers. Some say it is no coincidence that this area is home of Leonardo's *The Last Supper.* The title of the work is a warning to eaters-out who rely on two wheels to get home.

This restaurant in Via Brisa is surrounded by some very Milanese banks, and the remains of a distinctly Roman amphitheater. The décor is reminiscent of a trattoria, and its lacquered furniture, Spartan seating, and walled garden attract elegant diners. If you're looking for downmarket trattoria patrons, you need to look for imitation elegance. In Italian eateries, bad taste is a mark of authenticity. For example, it is important to examine the walls. If the pictures reveal a discriminating eye, distrust them. Much more reassuring are oils painted by a relative, the owner's daughter's landscapes, or still lifes by an enthusiastic cook.

You won't find the more extreme peaks of kitsch here, but other things merit attention. This is a restaurant where high-flying bankers come to meet A-list celebs, who come to rub shoulders with leading fashion designers, who want to bump into big names in the media, who come here to look down their noses at everyone else, only to beam in contentment when they're recognized. This little group has two things in common: a shared language and a shared palate, both razor-sharp and swift to dispense judgment.

It's one in the afternoon. In Milan, this is time for *la colazione,* which means breakfast in Rome but is the same thing as lunch in New York. The midday meal in Rome is *il pranzo,* which for many people in Milan means the evening meal that everyone in Naples calls *la cena.* Complicated? Sure it is. Italian catering is governed by laws that we take for granted but that aren't obvious. Food and drink are a perfect metaphor for Italy, offering a vast expanse of habits and exceptions for visitors to get lost in. Oh, we'll be there to give you a hand. But, like lifeguards after a rescue, we'll expect you to be grateful.

Consider the humble cappuccino. After ten o'clock in the morning, it is unethical, and possibly even unlawful, to order one. You wouldn't have one in the afternoon unless the weather was very cold. Needless to say, sipping a cappuccino after a meal is something only non-Italians do. Pizzas at midday are for schoolkids. Rice with meat is perfect, but pasta with meat is embarrassing unless it's cooked in the sauce. Having a starter after your pasta raises no eyebrows, but eating a main meat or fish dish instead of a starter looks greedy. Grating Parmesan over clams is an offense against religion, but if a young chef suggests it, express approval. Wine in flasks is for tourists—package tourists if the flask is hanging on the wall. Finally, there is garlic. Like elegance, garlic should be present but should not intrude. The *bruschetta* garlic toast served in some Italian restaurants abroad would be actionable in Italy.

Once, an English friend called this sort of thing "food fascism."

I told her she was exaggerating. She had ordered a cappuccino after her evening meal, and the waiter refrained from calling the police.

•  •  •

It has been said that the digestive tract is a metaphysical entity in Italy, like lawns in England. This is true, but our obsession is more serious. The English don't eat their lawns. We talk about food before we eat it, while we're eating it, and after we've eaten it. Digestive discussion reassures the stomach and prepares the mind—for another meal, and another discussion.

Gastronomy has become a passion that spills over into obsession. Every year, we spend fifty billion euros on eating out. The total includes unremarkable meals, but also some remarkable self-indulgences, a few confirmations, and one or two surprises. Here in Milan, a restaurant meal costs more than in Paris. Yet we continue to book, eat, drink, and pay up. Only to look at the check more closely afterwards, and protest.

We are the victims of our own good habits. Eating well in Italy is like hunting in a game reserve—it's hard to go wrong—but we also fall for marketing. Today restaurants always offer something else in addition to food, and charge for it. It might be visibility, confidentiality, innovation, tradition, aesthetics, nostalgia, provocation, or reassurance.

Recently, all things organic, natural, and rustic have been selling. Some adjectives work like perception-enhancing drugs. We started to eat green salad again when they gave it names like *rucola, radicchio, trevisana, chioggia, soncino, belga,* and *rughetta.* Olive oil has won its battle with butter, which has retired hurt. Even here, a certain minimalism endures. It is closely related to nouvelle cuisine, which satisfies the brain but not the stomach, and upsets the old-school Italian in all of us.

Many young chefs have realized this. They take traditional recipes and work on them. Almost invariably, the trick is to dress substantial ideas in light clothing. It is a worthy enterprise, for cooking is like a local dialect: use it or lose it. The risk is gastronomic snobbery. Fifty years ago, French philosopher Roland Barthes talked about the peasant meal as a rural fantasy of bored city-dwellers. We're in no hurry, but we're getting there.

This is clear from the fashion for florid menus. The simplest dishes have acquired incomprehensible names. Many restaurateurs cannot believe that all those words in the dictionary are free, so they go over the top. Do you remember the place in the Navigli district yesterday? You chose creamed vegetables, but the menu said *vellutata di verdure di stagione al profumo di finocchietto selvatico, servita coi crostini e olio extravergine d'oliva d'Abruzzo* (velouté of seasonal vegetables scented with wild fennel, served with croutons, and drizzled with extra-virgin Abruzzan olive oil), which is one way of charging ten euros for it. And what about *formaggio caprino avvolto nel controfiletto di bue, passato in padella, servito con le cipolle rosse di Tropea brasate* (goat's-milk cheese rolled in sirloin of beef, pan-browned, and served with braised red Tropea onions)? It was meat, cheese, and soaring violins.

Nowadays, an Italian menu is a short story, a certificate of origin, and a declaration of intent. Every so often, I read the translation to get an idea of what will be on the plate. "Shrimps and beans roll" may be ungrammatical, but it's clearer than *fagottino croccante alla maniera dello chef con gamberi e fagiolini* (crispy pastry *à la manière du chef* with shrimps and green beans). "Sea trout and sea bass" is more honest than *treccia di trota salmonata e branzino con timballo al cumino* (braid of salmon trout and sea bass with cumin-perfumed timbale).

The Piedmontese singer-songwriter Paolo Conte protested:

*"Pesce Veloce del Baltico"*
*dice il menu, che contorno ha?*
*"Torta Di Mais" e poi servono*
*polenta e baccalà . . .*
*cucina povera e umile*
*fatta d'ingenuità*
*caduta nel gorgo perfido*
*della celebrità . . .*

"Baltic Fast Fish"
it says on the menu, what's it served with?
"Cornbread" and then there's "polenta and
    baccalà" . . .
plain, unpretentious cooking
made with simplicity
fallen into the treacherous maw
of fame . . .

The song sums up the risks we are running. But if the words are a sophisticated sweet, we can digest them. Until the check arrives. Then we realize that today, in the age of the euro, not even adjectives are free.

●  ●  ●

There is much talk of food and wine, but not enough about their context. An Italian restaurant includes various rituals that excite and perturb. Take the cover charge. I can see from your expression that you don't see the reason for the exotic little starter on the check. But you should thank us.

The *Zingarelli 2005* Italian dictionary defines *coperto* as "From the French *couvert,* from the Latin *coopertu(m): coperto,* in the sense of what covers the table." The entry continues, "The set of plates, cutlery, glassware, and the like required for one person at table." Hence "Place at table." And so "Fixed charge paid in a restaurant for each place at table." The dictionary doesn't tell us why, though. One definition of the adjectival use of *coperto* throws light on this minor mystery of the catering world. "*Coperto:* ambiguous, hidden, dissimulated." In short, they charge us and don't tell us why.

We Italians have stopped worrying about it. We look on the *coperto* as a traditional form of taxation, as inevitable as our television license, and as illogical as many other things in Italy. Non-Italians get hot under the collar. The *coperto* looks like a subterfuge, or a veiled threat, especially when it is associated with bread: *Pane e coperto* € *1.50.* But then there are America's punitive tips, a form of mandatory generosity that can be as much as 20 percent of the check. "Tipping" is an oxymoron that the United States has absorbed, but which troubles the sleep of visiting Europeans.

Still, I won't deny that the *coperto* is insidious. It appears and disappears like an underground karst river. Now you see it, now you don't. Some restaurants add the *coperto* to the service charge. Some waive it for groups but insist on it for couples. It's always there on the official receipt, provided there is an official receipt, which is not always the case. That's another thing that disturbs non-Italians. They can't understand why the restaurateur acts as if he is doing you a favor when he scribbles what you owe on a piece of paper. It's obvious that you're the one doing the favor. The restaurateur can keep the money off the books and save 40 percent in taxes.

Ask the restaurant owner next time. He (or she) will look at you like an offended artist. "What? You have enjoyed the delights of my table, and you're worrying about fiscal details? All right, have a *limoncello* on the house . . ." Because there's always *limoncello*. It's our peace pipe, after a battle which the restaurateur always wins.

●  ●  ●

Restaurant restrooms are mysterious. The first problem is locating them. The sign that says *Toilette* is the start of a treasure hunt. The object of your desires will be next to two identical doors marked *Privato*, the emergency exit and the door to the kitchen. One particularly Milanese variation is the spiral staircase that takes you down to the basement. After weaving your way past crates of mineral water, discarded dishwashers, and surprised kitchen staff, you finally come to the restroom.

Next you have to find the light switch, because sunlight has yet to reach that corner of the planet. Logically, the switch should be on your right as you go in. It never is. The switch is camouflaged. If the walls are white, the light switch will be white. If the walls are off-white, the switch will be the same shade. Sometimes the light is operated by an electric eye, and impending micturition is greeted by a neon glare, as if you were a burglar caught red-handed.

What about flushing? Well, I've counted eighteen different flushing actions, most of them camouflaged, ranging from side levers, vertical levers, wall-mounted buttons, and pedals to a cord hanging from the ceiling. For some time now, the fashion has been for a rubber hemisphere on the floor that you press with your foot. Only rarely does it work first time. You generally have to pump away as if you were inflating a beach mattress. So, if you hear a rhythmic panting sound from behind a closed door, don't worry. It's not furtive sex, just foreplay to flushing.

The last hurdle is the washbasin. Restroom taps are a sort of subtle joke. The hot water works, but the cold doesn't, or vice versa.

Here, too, you're supposed to locate and lift levers, turn little wheels, depress pedals, or trigger photocells. The most sadistic models only work if you keep a button pressed. This requires three hands, a powerful nose, or lightning-swift execution (press button, insert hands in stream of water, wash, and rinse in under four seconds). Frequently, of course, there are no paper towels left, the roller towel won't roll, or there is only a machine with a jet of warm air that barely dries the hairs on your wrists.

There you have Italian restrooms. Have a good trip into the bowels of catering. Come back soon, if you can.

### The store, the field of lost battles

When non-Italians talk about Italy, exaggeration is the rule. You swing straight from enthusiasm to desperation, with no restorative amazement breaks. Take Samuel Johnson, for example. He said, "A man who has not been in Italy, is always conscious of an inferiority." This is flattering, but frankly excessive. At worst, such a man wouldn't be able to find Pesaro on a map. A more interesting, if somewhat Tarantinoesque, comment comes from the poet Robert Browning: "Open my heart and you will see / Graved inside of it, 'Italy.' " In a sense, Browning foresaw the success of our national brand.

If you look at the clothes stores, you'll notice they are selling on the strength of the *Made in Italy* label, for now. But Italians never cease to astound. Apparently, some Italian manufacturers are lobbying the European Union in Brussels for the introduction of a *Made in the EU* brand that will replace *Made in Italy*. But what will shoppers in Tokyo say when they buy an Armani jacket and see *Made in the EU* on the label? Probably the Japanese equivalent of "Oh well," followed by a deep sigh. How will wealthy Americans react when they discover that both Prada and Vuitton bags are made in the same geographical area? With consternation. The Chinese will be happy, though. They'll be able to use the same label for all their imitations of Italian, French, and British products. Think of the economies of scale.

So why won't *Made in the EU* work? Well, a label is a guarantee, but it's also fantasy, reassurance, and evocation. The new proposal supplies none of the above. There are no guarantees, since the whiskey could come from Florence and the leather belt might be from Edinburgh. Consumers prefer things the other way round. The name evokes nothing, either, because, unlike the U.S.A., the EU for now is just an abbreviation. When Bruce Springsteen sings "Born in the U.S.A.," America's eyes mist over. If Paul McCartney were to croon "Born in the EU," it just wouldn't be the same. Yet Freehold, New Jersey, isn't any more exciting than Liverpool, England.

Some may object that strength lies in unity. We've standardized passports and the currency, so why not labels? There's an easy answer. In the bank, or at the Mexican, or Mauritanian, or Malaysian, or Moldovan border, the euro and the maroon EU passport give us more protection than their national equivalents (the same would of course be true of a single European army, so it's hard to see what we're waiting for). But in trade, Europe's strong suit is diversity. An Audi evokes Germany, Chablis has the savor of France, and top-quality leather is redolent of Italy, although some people can't wait to make all these products in Hong Kong.

●  ●  ●

But back to the store. To start with, no one will pester you. No one will coddle or make compliments. The self-serving blandishment that plays such a large part in other Italian activities is oddly absent in Milan's most fashionable boutiques. City-center storekeepers seem to bear no relation whatever to the hotel porters you have met, and make you wish they did.

Note the hospital-ward ambience of some of the shop interiors. There is an aura of metal, glaring white lights, and polished counters. The clothes are lined up like surgical instruments. Consider the empty spaces, the milky ceilings, the objects hanging on steel pegs. Observe the knots of diminutive black-garbed saleswomen who look more Japanese than the Japanese they are serving. I don't know how long this will last, but probably not very long.

Italy insists on being original, and if possible entertaining, even when it decides to be uncomplicated. The Fiat Cinquecento car and the Olivetti Lettera 22 typewriter had those characteristics, like some models of Tod's shoes or Dolce & Gabbana's early fashion collections. But these shops are as dull as the clothes they are trying to sell. When Milan tries to be New York, that's when the trouble starts.

What about the prices? Well, it's the same story as the restaurants. When the euro was introduced, lots of traders applied conversion rates that ranged from the imaginative to the scandalous. It may have been an attempt to differentiate local goods from the flood of imports from the East. But it did nothing for sales figures.

Not even the sign that says *Saldi* (Sale) helps very much. An Italian sale is an abstract concept. It may be a real discount, or simply a turn of phrase. There is nothing automatic about price reductions. They are applied to the individual, and some people even feel offended when they are offered. On the outskirts of empire, paying full price can still be a status symbol.

But anyone from America, where shopping is a sporting discipline and discounts are rigorously scientific (either there is a discount or there isn't), fails to understand, and declines to purchase. No problem, say the little nurses in black. There are always the Russians. Just double-check that their credit cards haven't expired.

* * *

There's another little difficulty, which is finding your way through the designer labels, brands, and fashions. The last time I counted, there were 206 stylists in Milan, each one burning with an *inordinata praesumptio alios superandi* (an "inordinate presumption of superiority over others"), as Thomas Aquinas used to say. Tom was a philosopher and a saint, perhaps because he didn't drop in on Via Montenapoleone at cocktail time.

But you have to try to understand, because fashion—particularly women's fashion—is one of the great Italian industries, involving fine craft-workers and the odd genius as well as quite a few charlatans. Shall we try to draw one or two conclusions? Let's see, now. Designers can be divided into three categories, when they have a moment to spare between takeovers, franchises, yacht trips, and expeditions to China. They come in Street Culturist, Rear Mirror Viewer, and Cutting Edger varieties.

Street Culturists get their inspiration from the squares, avenues, and sidewalks, especially in the suburbs, at night. They are the nighthawks of ready-to-wear fashion. Nothings slips past them. The leader of the movement was Gianni Versace. It is no coincidence that his sister, Donatella, looks like Batman's little sister. Cavalli and Dolce & Gabbana are not far behind. Their miniskirts are as short as rollneck collars, cleavages go down to the knees, and the fabrics are leopardskin or python. If a Street Culturist goes to the zoo, the snakes and big cats have hysterics. If their models ventured outside (un)dressed like that, they'd be on the cover of *Vogue*, or get picked up by the police.

Rear Mirror Viewers forge ahead with their eyes fixed firmly on the past. Trunks, family albums, old films, or literary classics—nothing is too old to be new. Prada and Gucci are turbocharged Rear Mirror Viewers. Valentino is a diesel version. Ferragamo and Zegna are Rear Mirror Viewers, but steam-driven. But the bionic Rear Mirror Viewer is Giorgio Armani, who manages to look ahead and behind at the same time, maintaining a Caribbean tan on both profiles.

And the Cutting Edgers? There's Moschino, although the only people who would dare wear his stuff are Lagos-based pop stars or Cuban gambling-house keepers. Krizia is a Cutting Edger, when she can be bothered. And there's Ferré. His women may look as if they have just stepped off a spaceship with a touch of travel sickness, but they're certainly not predictable.

Why am I telling you all this? Well, that way you can go into the shops—sorry, "showrooms"—and make profound comments. For the time being, comments cost nothing.

●  ●  ●

Fashion thinks it is sensuous, but other kinds of shopping in Italy are even more so. People want to look inside a table lamp, touch a suitcase, listen to an explanation, sniff a carpet, or sneak an olive and talk about the flavor. That's one reason why e-commerce hasn't taken off in Italy. There are some things you can't do on the Web. Italians are sensitive, curious, and diffident. We don't even like goods in sealed packages. We wonder what the cellophane is trying to hide from us.

For Italians, buying has to be a tactile experience. When it isn't, it's no fun. If we went to a cheese shop, we'd see fabulous cheeses displayed like jewels (the same goes for the prices). You'd realize that Italian shoppers want to be seduced. They want—sorry, *we* want—a moral justification for our impending surrender. When we go into the cheese store, we have defeat written all over our faces. We yield to a Ricotta, submit to a Taleggio, and run up the white flag before a Crescenza.

The self-indulgence of an aging society, peer pressures, image-driven desires, needs we have been persuaded to acknowledge, and office rivalry all urge us to acquire. E-commerce is more than mere calculation in the United States, too, but American mechanisms have a scientific side that is missing in Italy. Everything in an American mall is designed to entice the shopper, from the height of the goods on display to the lights, the music, the sequence of colors, and the tireless, automatic courtesy of the clerks. In Italy, seducing the customer is instinctive. It's a craft, not a science. The clerks haven't been taught to sell. They have the blood of generations of wily merchants flowing in their veins. One day obsequious, the next detached; now a hint of seduction, now an explanation; coolness in the morning, and empathy in the evening.

But not in the center of Milan. Here they play by other rules.

* * *

This is a shoe store in the Brera district. A woman has come in to buy a pair of shoes. The clerk makes no move. She leans on the cash register, observing. Then she says hello, but it's such an unfriendly eructation that the customer thinks the clerk has digestive problems.

The lady tries on a few shoes. At the fourth pair, the clerk is showing signs of impatience. "I'm wasting her time," thinks the customer, guiltily. After a quarter-hour, the customer is a little cowed. Half an hour later, her feet are tired, the floor is covered in empty shoeboxes, and the clerk's eyes are flashing bolts of lightning. The customer seeks a way out, but there is none. As soon as she puts on the shoes she was wearing when she came in, the truth will out. She isn't going to buy anything.

In the end, the lady decides to lie. She whispers, barely audibly, "I'll stop in again. I have to speak to my husband." The clerk stares at the shopper without pity. For years, she has been hearing that "I'll stop in again," but no one ever has. " 'I have to speak to my husband!' " the clerk thinks to herself. "That woman doesn't even tell her husband where she's going on holiday!"

The clerk is irritated, and makes no secret of the fact. She doesn't believe the customer really wanted a pair of shoes. She might just have been passing the time of day. As she heads for the door, the customer feels confused and worried. For a moment, she thinks she's going to be attacked from behind. Out in the street, she reflects, "I would have bought a pair of shoes if the girl had been a little more polite. Those moccasins were really nice." But she daren't go back in.

The clerk is back at the cash desk, inspecting her fingernails. Suddenly she smiles. "Hey," she says to the other clerk, "didn't you feel sorry for that woman? If I'm any judge, she was the kind of woman who runs her own business, but she still couldn't tell me, 'Look, I've tried lots of shoes, but I haven't found a pair I like. Sorry.' I'd have understood, wouldn't I?"

Now imagine what would happen in the States, in an ordinary shoe store, in an ordinary mall, on the outskirts of an ordinary city. The same Milanese woman goes in to buy a pair of shoes. The smiling clerk comes over and greets her, "Hi! How are you today?" She's so welcoming that the Milanese lady wonders whether they have met somewhere before.

The clerk asks the customer to sit down. She talks about the weather. She makes jokes. The customer tries twenty pairs of shoes, then another ten. The clerk maintains her poise. She proposes new styles, and makes an effort to keep smiling. Half an hour later, the customer decides there's nothing she likes. Slightly embarrassed, she hints that she wants to go. The clerk doesn't look annoyed. Sad, if anything. She says, "It's a pity you didn't find a pair you like, ma'am. But don't worry, and do come back to see us." At the door, the young American says, "Have a nice day!"

The lady from Milan is now bemused. For an instant, she wishes her daughter were more like the clerk. "Perhaps I should have bought something. After all, those moccasins were really nice." Ten minutes later, she's back. The clerk is waiting for her at the door. "Welcome back!" the clerk croons. When the customer emerges from the shop, she is carrying a bag with her new shoes. She walks off. At that point, the clerk stops smiling. She turns round, and says to her colleague, "Hey, Tracy, did you see that Eye-talian? What a pain! But I sold her those goddamn shoes. Can I sell shoes or can I *sell shoes?*"

Well, that's enough of that. Now let's take a look at having a good time, which in Italy is a serious business.

## The nightspot, where foxes turn into peacocks

Unlike my computer, my country hasn't got a reset button. But it does have the night. Since time began, Italy has used the dark to reset, restart, recharge, and repose from the challenging task of being Italian.

On the terrace in summer, at the fireside in winter, and in pizza restaurants, clubs, trattorias, and nightspots all year round, the evening in Italy is official consolation time, a moment off the leash, and the daily slot for R & R. The night is a legal drug, and free of the alcohol-driven inebriation it induces in other countries. We're not out to get wasted. We want to carry on piecing together our unpredictable mental architectures. The sky and the weather help. Italy's climate is an instigation to indulge. If we had Scottish weather in Italy, there would have been several revolutions. Instead, we lodged the occasional protest, made a lot of promises, and talked.

Remember those people at the restaurant? They weren't shouting. The same thing happens here. At a certain hour of the day, the noisiest country in Europe lowers its voice and takes a break. The social shrieks in a German *Stube* are inconceivable in an Italian eatery. The *Stube* noise is too loud for conversation, and we are a nation of talkers. In all that bedlam, we wouldn't be able to appreciate what's on our plate, or in our glass. And Italians over the age of twenty-five are fastidious tasters of food, drink, and situations.

•  •  •

This is Bastioni di Porta Volta. The bar we are in is long, narrow, and looks as if it is moored in the middle of the Milan traffic. It used to be a shelter for streetcar drivers, but for the past ten years it's been a fashionable nightspot, with tiny round tables, drapes, sofas, glass, antique lamps, and gilt picture frames. The shift concept has remained, though. At one in the afternoon, the office workers flood in, with not much money and even less time. At eight in the evening, it's the turn of the apéritif drinkers, who make a dinner out of the bar snacks. Then come the people of the night. And the night is unusual and instructive, like almost everything in Italy.

•  •  •

Lesson number one: people come here to drink, not to get drunk. Italians like being merry, but barfing on the sidewalk is not considered the high point of Saturday evening, as it often is north of the Alps.

Recently, though, the goalposts have been moving. In a whirlwind exchange of defects, Southern Europe is drinking younger, more, and worse, while Northern Europe is getting more temperamental and less predictable. But there's a long way to go yet. In Italy, we're still well qualified to offer courses on the theory and practice of alcohol consumption.

To start with, there is no legal age limit for drinking—or, if there is, no one seems aware of it. Families have the duty of educating children to drink, and for now the bottle is not an object of desire but a managed, pleasure-inducing habit.

Not all foreigners realize this. The Italian businessman who has a glass of wine with his lunch is frowned at by his American (or German, or Dutch, or Scandinavian) colleague, from behind a glass of mineral water. But at the end of the evening, the former will be helping the latter back to the hotel, where, after overdoing the gin-and-tonics, vermouths, wines, and pousse-cafés, the foreigner will attempt to ransack the minibar.

It is curious to note that we rarely boast about this self-control. We don't use the endemic alcoholism of certain Northern European countries to humiliate them when they judge us. It's not a problem. Everyone has a right to intervals of bad behavior, which deserve comprehension, not cruelty.

●　●　●

Lesson number two is economic. A doubtfully tinted, improbably named cocktail costs ten euros. Today is Saturday. Factor in dinner for two at a restaurant and the total for the evening comes to more than one hundred euros. A schoolteacher earns thirteen hundred euros a month, so it follows that you won't see many schoolteachers in here. A wholesaler earns that much in a day, or a week, depending on the trade, turnover, and degree of compliance with the tax regime. That means there will be some wholesalers in here, camouflaged among the drinkers with rich parents.

What's going on? The answer is simple, even if no one will admit it. The introduction of the euro caused an economic earthquake. Everybody knows that, whatever the official figures say, tenthousand-lire price tags in Milan became ten euros, although they should have turned into about half that sum. Was it the fault of government, or did ordinary people just miss something? It doesn't matter now. What is clear is that the earthquake opened up a gaping chasm, and many middle-class Italians fell into it.

The survivors were the professional class and the self-employed, who were able to crank up their prices. Into the rift went Italians with a salary, who have to spend it just to survive. For the first time, thirty-somethings are worse off than their parents, or if they are better off it is only thanks to what their parents have managed to save in the form of family homes or seaside apartments. In 1970, a middle manager, the kind they call a *quadro* in Italy (the name also means "picture," but they don't hang them on the wall yet), could buy an automobile with the equivalent of six months' earnings. Today it takes twelve. Look at the cars parked outside. They cost fifty thousand euros. An office worker would have to work for four years to buy one, provided he or she slept rough and didn't eat.

Would you like to know how much the owners of the cars declare on their tax return? Anything from twenty thousand to two hundred thousand euros. It depends on their customers, their accountant, and their conscience.

You will say, Why doesn't the government do something? Why not cross-check vehicle ownership with tax returns? The answer is that the government doesn't want to. Controllers and controlled have an unspoken agreement. You don't change, we don't change, and Italy doesn't change, but we all complain that we can't go on like this. Perhaps on a night like tonight, when Milan costs a fortune but otherwise is not that bad.

* * *

Lesson number three is emotional. Italians are as sharp as foxes in a restaurant, but in a place like this we turn into peacocks. The transformation is curious zoologically, but anthropologically explicable.

Look at the guy over there. He moves around wearing a self-satisfied smirk, he admires himself in the mirrors, and he flashes a dazzling smile at the girls. There is a courtship ritual that some people abroad think is an extension of the Latin-lover technique. Wrong. The Latin lover had determination. He was an actor, a lifeguard, or a rich kid. Often he wasn't terribly bright, but the absence of self-doubt fueled his self-esteem. Today the seducer is a tortured soul. He is just as enthusiastic a hunter, but he is less ambitious, and he has one or two poignant touches of vanity. The shaven head camouflages incipient baldness, and the generous cut of the beach shirt disguises a potbelly.

But he is still an interesting specimen. The combination of voice, eyes, hands, and costume is pleasing. Italian charm exists. It is an ability to seduce that needn't necessarily be sexual. It works between human beings in much the same way a modem talks to a server. The two systems shake hands and establish a communication protocol.

The degree of understanding that in Germany takes all evening, and in Britain requires cohabitation, is lightning-fast in Italy. Remember the hotel porter? It takes him seconds to get a handle on his clients. This tattoo-bedecked barman only needs half a minute. Go and order something to drink. He'll be sizing you up as he pours your rum on the rocks. He just needs to register your clothes and your expression. He'll note every slight hesitation, what you order, and how you order it. He'll observe what you do and don't do. You might think we're only getting a drink. So? That's more than enough.

What's the problem? Well, this instant understanding can easily become complicity. Let's take a Milanese example, since we're in Milan. Silvio Berlusconi is the most talked-about Italian abroad. He certainly knows how to convince people, it seems. They say he has amazing powers of seduction. I can believe it, but it's *simpatia* taken to pathological extremes. The idea that you can persuade any-body—from a British reporter to a German chancellor, a Russian president, or an Italian electorate—with a smile and a bit of fudging is a dangerous one.

If you were to say as much to Silvio Berlusconi, how would he react? He wouldn't take it badly. In fact, he wouldn't take it at all. He'd put a hand on your shoulder, let you know he was offended, and try to understand why communication had broken down. Did he get one of the handshaking protocols wrong? Which one?

# Day Three: Still in Milan

The condominium, a vertical space for oblique
obsessions

Milan is a city that we use a lot but see very little. You're new here, so take a look around. You note balconies, corners, cubes, satellite dishes, windows, roofs, terraces, façades, and minor building violations condoned first by amnesties, and then by force of habit. Italy is also a multilayered jungle of colors, lit up by the Sunday-morning sunshine.

The architect Renzo Piano says that he lived in Florence as a boy but found it "too boring, because it was too perfect." Milan, on the other hand, "was the least perfect, and therefore the most interesting, city." That's the way it has stayed. It's still interesting, and even less perfect.

I don't want to convince you that these buildings in Via Foppa are lovely, but you'll have to understand them to judge them. They are the guileless triumph of the first buds of prosperity after war's devastation. They explain Milan, and Milan explains and anticipates Italy. The Risorgimento, socialism, fascism, anti-fascism, the resistance, the economic boom, the culture of kickbacks and the magistrates' Clean Hands reaction, Bettino Craxi's champagne socialists, Umberto Bossi's Northern League, soccer, fashion, publishing, television, advertising, and information technology all started here. Someone behind those unsightly blinds dreamed it all up.

OK, Milan is not a beautiful city, but, despite its surly expression, it's imaginative, open to contaminations, and constantly busy. Those of us who work here love Milan the way we might love a relative's uneven teeth: that's the way they are, and they've done a lot of chewing. I don't expect you to see Milan in the same way. Urban orthodontics is a personal affair. But do take a look at Milan. The walls are dirty, and the streets are jammed, but it's worth it.

* * *

A midday meal with friends. Don't expect a penthouse. You'll see an apartment, Italy's most popular, and revealing, dwelling type. One Italian in four lives in a building like this one, which sprang up in the 1960s. There are all sorts of names for them—*condominio, palazzo, palazzina, stabile,* or *caseggiato*—but they all mean "apartment block." Even today, most new homes are apartments. In the United Kingdom, apartments constitute only 15 percent of the housing stock. In other words, London is a roof, but Milan is a balcony.

Why is it important to understand places like this? Because the apartment building—the *condominio*—is the reverse of the piazza, or square. It's the dark side of the Italian head. The piazza is where the individual rebels, the place you go to meet other people. But the *condominio* is your alibi from society, the place where you can shut yourself away and don't have to see anyone. The proximity of others becomes a source of annoyance: those noises on the far side of the wall, the elevators that never arrive, the drips from the balcony above, and the squeaks in the night. The *condominio* is an incubator of delirium, which is interesting when it's someone else's.

Dino Buzzati understood this in 1963, when he published *Un amore* (*A Love*), a novel about buildings. Buzzati's Milan is magical and mysterious, a sort of Hogwarts for grown-ups where anything can happen ("All around, still motionless in the rain, the big city that will soon wake up and start to gasp for breath, to struggle, to twist, to charge back and forth alarmingly in order to do, undo, sell, earn, and dictate, for an infinite number of mysterious desires and fixations . . ."). But at least in those days people in apartment blocks spoke to one another. Neighbors swapped sugar and information the way they do in America. The only difference was that they swapped across a landing instead of a picket fence. Then something happened. The *condominio* lost its social role, becoming merely a place people lived, became suspicious, and complained in. Only the occasional TV sitcom fosters the myth of a joyously shared living space. But that's a form of nostalgia. When a social phenomenon reaches the small screen in America, it's a snapshot. In Italy, it's a funeral.

＊　＊　＊

Our apartments—they average one hundred square meters (about one thousand square feet)—are our nests. Think of squirrels. They find a nice hole in a tree, fill it with provisions, and spend the winter there. We do the same. We surround ourselves with possessions, shut ourselves in behind security doors, and hunker down to listen to the world through the walls. Every so often, we argue with the other squirrels.

In order to understand the grim meticulousness we invest in some of these squabbles, you have to know the legal definition of a *condominio*. According to the Italian Civil Code, it is a "special form of community property expressed in the jointly owned parts of a building." It cannot be dissolved, which is why the communal ownership is described as *forzosa*, "forced." The adjective fits like a glove. It is the obligatory element that makes living together so complicated. In America, neighbors may fall out because of a poorly mown lawn, Germans might complain about offensive odors, the British bristle over untrimmed hedges, and the Swiss will object to an unruly dog. But in Italy, apartment dwellers have a whole arsenal of excuses for a fight.

Here's a list. There is the division of shared expenses, which generates suspicion. Accidental damage can look like an affront. Infiltrations can stimulate the wildest flights of fancy. Badly parked cars irritate those who get home late. Then there are offensively located satellite dishes, garbage in the wrong place, and doors that go bang in the night.

The *condominio* generates new categories of humanity. There's the Crafty Co-Owner who doesn't turn up at meetings, ensuring there is no quorum. There's the Condominium Lawyer, who almost never has a law degree. He only has a sprinkling of legal jargon, and turns up at meetings with the Civil Code under his arm. There's the Shortsighted Apartment Owner, who only sees the burnt-out lightbulb if it's outside her own front door. There's the Rabble-Rouser, who stirs up Staircase A against Staircase B, claiming obscure but unimpeachable rights and titles. The interesting thing is that someone always listens.

Finally, there is the Litigious Lady, who has learned the condominium regulations by heart. She screams, "I want everything I say
to be recorded in the minutes!" and then takes everyone to court.
The judge almost always orders the parties to pay their own legal
costs, so she ends up losing money. But the Litigious Lady doesn't
care. Going to court gives her a reason to live. I once heard of an entire condominium that was taking legal action against the tenant on
the top floor. He was worried about the costs of natural-gas heating, so he had built a fireplace and installed a hoist to haul up the
wood he chopped at night in his garage. With a chainsaw. It sounds
like the start of a horror story. I'd love to know how it ended.

*   *   *

The condominium is a space of continuous, compulsory solidarity,
but we Italians only like the voluntary kind, from time to time. In a
place like this, even the elderly learn to fight. A curious generational
war develops. It's youth against age, and age generally has more
combat experience. Older residents use their knowledge of the terrain—they don't go out to work, so they have time to carry out inspections and watch what goes on—and are always ready for a fight.
If push comes to shove, they shove with gusto. The lady on the first
floor complains about the cost of the pest-control service, and re-
placing the door phone-intercom panel. The couple on the fourth
floor won't pay for the inspection and unblocking of the kitchen-
waste pipes. Little things like these fill people's lives.

Of course, some pensioners don't distinguish workdays from
holidays. In fact, many appear not to distinguish day from night.
They will undertake any activity at any time of day. The locks on
their doors are the heavy-duty variety, and open with Gothic creaks
when everyone else is asleep. Their spoiled and much-loved dogs

bark when they shouldn't, and do their business where they oughtn't. Children, adored and beyond criticism in Italy, are the cause of endless arguments. Their games become terrorist attacks; their shrieks of joy grate on the nerves.

Finally, there is the condominium elevator, where we exercise our incommunicability. We don't like enforced intimacy. We dread talking about the weather. We are annoyed by the cooking smells, the stench of cigarettes furtively smoked, and the perfume of the woman who used the lift before us. We dislike the scratches beside the fourth-floor button, and try to avoid the elevator mirror that inspects us in the morning and judges us in the evening. We do not dislike the sense of complicity in an anonymous elevator, though the predictability of its domestic ascents and descents disturbs us. But we cannot avoid the elevator. The other option is using the stairs, and that would never do.

### The eat-in kitchen, the nerve center of domestic counterespionage

Fifty years ago, T. S. Eliot wanted to understand what the components of English culture were. The interest is typical of those who have become English but were not born that way. Eliot scribbled down this list: "Derby Day, Henley Regatta, Cowes, the twelfth of August, a cup final, the dog races, the pin table, the dart board, Wensleydale cheese, boiled cabbage cut into sections, beetroot in vinegar, nineteenth-century Gothic churches and the music of Elgar."

Three years ago, two American humorists, Rob Cohen and David Wollock, listed "101 Great Reasons to Love Our Country." They started with freedom, the Constitution of the United States, and apple pie, going on to Times Square, Route 66, Sam Adams beer, Las Vegas, and breast implants, and then threw in Madonna and light switches that actually work.

Could we compile such a list for Italy? It would be wiser not to, which is why we'll try. My list would include Baroque, knowing the right people, titles, cell phones, abstract nouns, Vespas, deck shoes, parking, sweaters draped over the shoulders, espresso, and the living room. Actually, I'd put the living room first. It's the political and geographical hub of the Italian home. It's the nerve center of Italy's grand design. The country's fate is decided in the living room. Ministries and boardrooms are only there to tidy up the details.

•   •   •

Twenty-two million households. Twenty-two million living rooms. Some people still call such a room a *tinello* (eat-in kitchen). The name is out of date, which means it's interesting. It's a diminutive of *tino*, the container used to carry grapes at harvesttime. Then the name was transferred to the room where the servants ate together. Nowadays, vintages are planned scientifically, domestic help works freelance, and *tinello* just means the room next to the kitchen. In other words, it's a small dining room. It's too shy to call itself a living room, and too practical to use just for meals.

In recent years, the eat-in kitchen–cum–living room has edged out the reception room of the better-off (who never used it), and the kitchen of the poor (who used it too much). There's a TV set, a sofa, two armchairs, coffee-table books, cushions, stereo, ornaments, pets, and polemics. The *tinello*—vaguely related to the Victorian drawing room, where the lady of the house received visitors—is no longer a female domain. Modern Italian males tend to take an interest in activities that were traditionally reserved for women, such as arranging the furniture, choosing the drapes and upholstery. Men always have a firm opinion and questionable taste.

That's another reason why the eat-in kitchen–cum–living room is worth studying. It is the focus of the Italian family, just as the kitchen is the nerve center of the Russian or American household. It's the place where the family talks about everything, all the time, from births to weddings, schools, vacations, expenses, and things to purchase. Children's education begins—when it does begin— around a table laid for dinner. When a couple splits up—which happens quite a lot, especially here in northern Italy—it is in the *tinello* that the partners argue, state their points of view, and try to salvage what they can.

Think about the Italian families you know. Have you noticed how much they talk? Too much, some might say. OK, but at least they talk. In the English-speaking world, many families communicate via adhesive notes on the refrigerator. Everyone has his or her own separate life, and grabs something to eat in between attending courses and meetings at school. Not in Italy. Around an Italian table, people reason, argue, and learn to defend (or change) their points of view.

This is what the London *Observer* has to say: "The idea of regular meals in the company of their parents, let alone spending a minute longer under the familial roof than they have to, seems to be repellent to the average Briton under thirty, seeking independence, self-expression and sexual adventure. [Italians] sit around the table, regularly, once a day or at least several times a week. They learn how to manage a knife and fork, how to behave and how to talk. Consequently, young Italians are, by and large, gracious, well-mannered and fluent."

Many Italians might say, "It's not fair! Foreigners criticize us for our politics, our corruption, and our television, and then praise us just for our family life?" "Just"? Knowing how to behave in company, behaving politely, and communicating easily are substantial qualities. We should keep them in mind, and be proud of them. We don't get the chance very often.

•   •   •

So the family is a counseling service and a Talmudic school. And that's not the end of it. In fact, it's only the beginning.

The family is a bank. Loans for first homes almost invariably come from parents. There are no formalities, no interest, and quite often no obligation to repay the capital. Subsequent loans, for vacations, cars, and other major expenses, are also not uncommon. Does this create psychological dependence? Well, it depends on the personality of the borrowers and the wisdom of the lenders. Still, it's an alternative to American-style premature adult debt.

The Italian family is a form of insurance coverage with no policy to sign, premiums to pay, or small print to read. In case of emergency, parents and relatives kick in. Nearly all of them ask few questions. Some, however, ask lots. There's no way out. The questions have to be answered. The only rule is that you can't switch insurers.

The Italian family is an employment agency. One Italian in three admits to finding a job through relatives. Half of Italy's engineers, 40 percent of dentists, and 25 percent of notaries inherited their profession. It's less than ideal for competition and social mobility. But at least it creates family traditions, and permits savings on brass nameplates and headed notepaper.

The Italian family is a market where nothing is sold, lots of stuff is given away, and everything is haggled over. Nephews and nieces stand in as drivers. Uncles and aunts help pay for their cell phones. The son fixes the intercom, but doesn't have to pay for leaving his car in his parents' garage. The next-door neighbor walks the daughter's dog, and her father, who's a nurse, will drop round when the neighbor needs an injection. Swaps of goods and services, horticulture, and minirevivals of the feudal economy complement the systematic recycling of clothing, tools, and furniture. Italy's ancient solidarity, the type that people, depending on mood and circumstance, either like or feel stifled by, has become more sophisticated. The family is now its hub.

The Italian family was once a residential-care home. When Italy was an agricultural society, there was always space for the old. Today Italy's homes have shrunk, and with them the patience of their occupants. Not everyone has the space or desire to live with an aging parent, but the care home is an option people are reluctant to adopt. Those who can afford one seek an apartment nearby. This has perked up the real-estate market—eight Italians in ten are owner-occupiers, a record for Europe—and produced a series of side effects. Granny across the landing can, if necessary, stand in as a babysitter or cook, water the plants, or look after the dog. Her pension means she can contribute to the family budget. A sixteen-year-old's Vespa might be a gift from Granny, who may also finance the social life of a wage-deprived twenty-five-year-old. You could object that this is unemployment benefit under another name. It is. But it arrives via Granny's purse, and makes her feel important.

Surprised? Hold on, because there's more. The family is an infirmary. It's the place where flu-blighted Italian males crawl for shelter, glowering like wounded animals. The family is a hotel, with round-the-clock room service, a TV in your room, and an efficient laundry.

The family used to be a restaurant where you didn't have to reserve a table. Now it's a sort of snack bar where you can always get something to eat (in 1950, the average Italian housewife spent seven hours in the kitchen; today it's forty minutes). It's a dormitory when you're in college (average age at graduation—twenty-eight), and a bachelor pad for those between relationships.

Finally, an Italian family is a news service. Many mothers have a landline phone, camera phone, fax, e-mail, terrace with a panoramic view, field agents, good hearing, and marvelous intuition. This means they can always locate their children, nephews, and nieces. There's really no need for a counterespionage service in Italy. All we need is a hundred or so fully equipped moms.

* * *

Grandparents who won't let go and invasive parents produce *mammoni*, mother-fixated children afraid to fend for themselves. When foreigners arrive in Italy, this is one of the things they know, just as they know that Venice is damp and the tower in Pisa leans.

*Mammoni* is a word non-Italians love. You love all those "m"s, that orotundity, the literature, and the hint of reproach laced with envy. Do *mammoni* actually exist? Of course they do. They exist, they exaggerate, and they're even more interesting than you imagine.

For a start, it's true that half of Italy's parents cohabit with adult children. The figure for Spain is the same, whereas in other European countries the proportion is lower, with 34 percent in France, 28 percent in Austria, 26 percent in Great Britain, and 19 percent in Norway. The United States is even further behind, with only 17 percent.

A first consideration might be that it's obvious why there are so few births in Italy and Spain. How can you do the necessary while your family is watching Saturday-evening TV on the other side of the wall? It's an operation that requires concentration, even in Milan or Madrid.

Italy's *mammoni* point to other extenuating circumstances. There aren't enough homes to rent, it's hard to find a job, and a new family costs. I'd add to the list the agreeably irresponsible lifestyle—encouraged by television, blessed by advertising, and tolerated by society—that in recent years has produced a new category of individual, the twenty-first-century parentally modified (male) *neo-mammone*. The tenacious youthfulness of Mom and Dad has relieved the *neo-mammone* of responsibility. At the age of thirty-something, today's *neo-mammone* is the descendant of filmmaker Federico Fellini's aimless youngsters in *I vitelloni (The Young and the Passionate)*, but with more money and less imagination. The *neo-mammone* is polite, but can turn arrogant if contradicted. He will admit to narcissism, but only because he likes the sound of the word. This long-distance adolescent lives in a morass of technology, plans for holidays in faraway places, and sporting enthusiasms. He has an epic vision of himself. His anthem is a fine pop song by Vasco Rossi, "Vita spericolata" ("Reckless Life"), "And then we'll meet like movie stars, for a whiskey at the Roxy Bar." It doesn't matter if the Roxy Bar is in a shopping mall, or if he has to sneak back into the apartment without waking Dad after risking life and limb on the drive home.

● ● ●

Not all young Italians are like that, luckily, or the country would have ground to a standstill long ago. Most youngsters are not dependent on their parents. Let's say they respect them, fear them, and manipulate them, according to circumstance.

The English-speaking world's solution—wave the kids off to

college, then see them only on holidays, unless there are disasters or fits of remorse—fails to convince Italy's twenty- and thirty-somethings. It's also not very practical, given the difficulty of finding a job or a place to rent.

In these cases, the compromise is utilitarian yet poetic. Many young people create an all-Italian melting pot, in apartments where a graduate from Milan lives with two students from Bari and a sales rep from Rome, who sublets to a construction worker from Brescia. These are places where spring-cleaning is put off until October, food is stored in the freezer, pasta with tuna is cooked in a dozen different ways, and a glass is raised for every celebration because it costs too much to go out for a drink.

They are the frozen-food generation. These young people say they have "decamped," an expression that reflects a healthy mental nomadism. Yet they have not turned their backs on their families. They know the power and the benefits of the eat-in kitchen they grew up in. Witness the dirty laundry, guiltily handed over on arrival and lovingly returned on departure. The mums—the Tupperware Generation?—cook ready meals. Just heat it up, they say with a professional smile. Dads help with the rent. Grandparents, uncles, and aunts contribute to the cell phone bill, provided they get a call every so often.

If all goes well, a few years later these young Italians enter the next stage, of insecure jobs, a little discretionary cash, an exhausting social life, a first home, and heroic attempts to furnish it. Style? Just one: enforced minimalism with a Scandinavian touch. In this IKEA society, everyone has the same bookshelves, the same sofa, the same beds, and the same shower curtains. In fact, that's one reason why these young men and women feel right at home when they visit with one another. Sometimes they don't bother leaving.

It's a new Italian family, and someone ought to study it.

The bedroom, the bathroom, and how hard it is to
find a space of your own

If we had a bird's-eye view of Italy and zoomed in, as in the opening scene of *American Beauty,* we'd see a land not far from the sea.
Then we'd see a town, a neighborhood, a building, an apartment, a
living room, and a bedroom. It is there that two Italians—alone,
apart, or in various permutations—demonstrate for their unseen
observer the keynotes of Italy's intimate moments. These are, in order of importance, self-indulgence, overcrowding, and fatigue.

● ● ●

The "strange multitude of little things necessary" that consoled Robin-
son Crusoe can also be found in an Italian bedroom. It's the same blend
of found and brought objects, with the same striving for self-sufficiency.
On Crusoe's island, the objects were a rope, a piece of cloth, and a
knife. In the bedroom, they include a television set and DVD player,
alarms, cell phones recharging, watches, palmtops, laptops, and
mini–music centers. The mysterious depths of our wardrobes enable
us each morning to construct a semblance of our self-image. The mirror tells us how things have gone.

An apartment, noted the French writer Julien Green in the
1960s, is a forest with clearings, quiet rooms, then "zones of horror"
and "crossroads of fear." Little has changed. The horror of the common zones remains, and though the rooms are still quiet, they have
been filled with gear and new functions. Frenzied restructuring has
created columns of vertical incomprehension. A bedroom on the
second floor is under a bathroom on the third, a living room on the

fourth, another bathroom above that, and on the sixth a room where the owner indulges in some noisy hobby like politics or popular music.

The suppression of the corridor has extended the children's room, which today is a technological powerhouse where infant Italians console themselves for not having any space to fill with their imagination. Computers, PlayStations, iPods, and other electronic wizardry occupy the tables and shelves. Nowadays, every corner has to be used for something. For want of anything better, it can serve as a dumpsite.

* * *

I'm not the only person interested in the waste products of the Western world. Seagulls, garbage collectors, and Don DeLillo share my fascination, as does Paul McCartney ("Buy Buy / Says the Sign in the Shop Window / Why Why / Says the Junk in the Yard" ["Junk," 1970]). Overconsumption is not an Italian exclusive, it's the chronic malaise of every sated society. But, as usual, we Italians add a pinch of imagination.

Once upon a time, homes had attics and cellars. Now, if you're lucky, they have a garage, but that's for cars. Occasionally, you find a sort of burial niche in the basement, protected by grilles and padlocks. Attics have been converted into penthouse living spaces, with horrendous, city-council-approved dormers that deface the rooftop skyline.

And so things that are being stored—for a birthday, to be recycled, a New Year, or a fashion to come round again—end up in the odd corners of our apartments. They are, as it were, the earwax of the home. It's not elegant to talk about them, but they're there. Two, three, or four of everything. But you can't keep four hair dryers, purchased in 1988, 1994, 1996, and 2001, unless you want to organize an Exhibition of Domestic Hair Dessication.

Try to explain this to some families, though. They won't listen. Embalming the recent past is the national sport of the middle classes. Homes show how many millions of conservatives there are in Italy. We may well keep certain individuals in Parliament for the same reason we hang on to the soft toys we had as children: they're getting threadbare, but we can't live without them.

The modern "multiple-location attic" is first and foremost a construct of the mind, not a physical space. The discarded gadgets, the multiple cassettes, the plethora of mugs, the brooding ovenware, the superannuated ski boots, and the user manuals for useless products are all tucked away in any available space. Pensioned-off Nativity scenes, junior-high textbooks, the baskets Christmas gifts came in, boxes of every conceivable configuration and color, synthetic-fiber blankets, ancient battery-chargers, tangles of black cable, a turntable, envelopes, and recipe books find a home in the new Italian attic that is everywhere and nowhere.

Many cultures, America's in particular, regard moving home as a moment of catharsis. In the U.S., people throw things out when they move. We don't move very often—only one Italian in five has moved in the past ten years, half the European average—and we hold on to everything. We live in the museum of our own past. One of these days, we're going to have to pay ourselves to get back in.

•  •  •

Yet, no matter how jam-packed Italian homes are, they look very predictable to many foreigners. This is particularly true of bedrooms. In Northern Europe, bedrooms are bastions of anarchy in well-ordered societies; in Italy, they are an orderly refuge in a land of chaos. It is as if we were all expecting an inspection that never comes. An American goes into her bedroom and slings her suitcase on the bed. An Italian won't, afraid of some mysterious infection. You're more likely to find a child in an Italian's bed than a breakfast. Parents prefer children, provided they don't leave crumbs.

Parquet floors contribute to the impression of order. Once parquet was only for urban living rooms, but now it has penetrated the remotest provincial bedrooms. British-style carpets are regarded with suspicion as potential magnets for dirt. Linoleum, that promise of modernity in the 1950s, nowadays covers only the farthest corners of our memory. The tiles that shine proudly in so many eat-in kitchens are covered by rugs to take the edge off the graveyard cold they leave on the eye and the soles of the feet, two very sensitive areas of the Italian physique.

Then there's the bathroom. It's more stylish than a French bathroom, more comfortable than its American equivalent, wider than a British one, more imaginative than its German peer, and more often used than a Dutch bathroom: in Amsterdam, they rinse their hands under the kitchen tap; in Milan, we dash to the bathroom, as if the running water in other rooms weren't quite as clean. It is in the bathroom that we seek ab(so)lution from our sins. There's no other explanation for the amount of time we spend there. Some Italians go in for interminable ablutions, but most of us meditate, surrounded by the paraments of the profane: matching hand towels, essences, reading matter, and a range of identical sprays. As a result, we risk washing our hair with shaving cream, or shaving with deodorant.

The bathroom furnishings are decided after heated discussion in the family. There is a broad national consensus on what fixtures to install—an odd-shaped washbasin, a sensuous-looking toilet bowl,

tub with shower, and of course a bidet—but families still fall out
over the tiling. Everyone knows that errors in this area are impossible to correct. The wrong tiles will be staring at you for years, re-
minders of a long-gone flight of fancy.

Manufacturers know this, and take advantage. Their catalogues
read like esoteric manuals, proffering Goa Blues, Shadow Greens,
and Mesopotamia Reds. Showrooms are places of perdition, where
Mom loses track of time and Pop loses his temper. Then an
armistice is signed, in the shape of a blue tile, four inches square,
that carries a double discount. It is entirely unremarkable, and the
retailer is selling it off cheap to get rid of it.

* * *

You'll want me to tell you what two Italians who share no blood ties
do in the bedroom when they're in there together. This is the
threshold on which historians have hesitated, but they were the only
ones. Novels, magazines, film, TV, and neighbors have examined the
question in detail, and know almost all there is to know.

It turns out that couples in bed sleep, watch television, phone,
argue, read, and make love. That's more or less the order of time
spent on these activities, although some authorities maintain that
reading comes after making love—not so much because there's a
surfeit of lovemaking as because there's a lack of bedside reading
material.

Are we embarrassed to talk about this? Not any longer. We're
sorry to have to disappoint our guests' expectations, but the once-
prudish Italian nation has changed its habits, and its undergarments.
Those young black-clad Sicilian women now exist only in TV commercials. Girls in Milan show off their belly buttons, their love affairs, and their parents' discomfiture. It's not clear which they enjoy

revealing most. Their male contemporaries are scared at first, then adjust. Moms tell their friends and the papers about their problems in bed. Dads say nothing, and work out their fantasies on the Web.

Regarding sex, Italy is now a province of Europe, and has little in common with America. As you know, social sensuality is nonexistent in the U.S. Over there, modesty is the official norm and pornography is an industry, but little light is shed on the vast space in between. In Washington, working women wear suit-shaped body armor, and defend it with flashing eyes. In offices in Milan, they talk about sex the way they talk about balance sheets. One person drafts, another audits, and a third expresses doubts about the auditor.

We are not yet rational about some things, but we do want to look relaxed. So some go too far, and no one has the heart to tell them. On Italian TV, women are exhibited like poultry at the butcher's. Commercials tempt us with women in cages, like cockatoos. You read and hear people say that all this makes Italy exciting. I fear it will lead to disaster. Many surveys, and lots of female friends, tell me that the men are uncertain and under stress.

Who knows, we may end up envying an America that is scared of a wardrobe malfunction at the Super Bowl, or Sharon Stone crossing her legs. America is still capable of getting worked up, and doesn't play computer games in bed.

·

# Day Four: Toward Tuscany

The train, where many talk, few listen, and everyone
understands

Stations disclose an interesting Italy. There is a stratification of habits and memories that the Italian railway company has decided not to disturb. Efficiency has suffered, but the atmosphere has benefited enormously.

There's something old-fashioned about the uniforms, the loosened ties, and the sad-looking staff moving around behind the glass like fish in an aquarium. There's something touching about the souvenirs on sale at Milan's Stazione Centrale. The gondolas, shells, saints, Virgin Marys, cathedrals, and lucky charms are an Italy that we Italians find hard to understand, but which consoles foreigners because it confirms the image you already have in your eyes: it's a neorealist film that doesn't require tiresome updates.

Ah, Milan's Stazione Centrale! Usually, out-of-towners think it's memorable, and they're quite right. Once you've seen it, how can you forget it? I confess that I, too, quite like the building. It's out of proportion—an interlude of imperialism in a business-focused town. But it doesn't look too bad. When I can, I raise my eyes, keeping a firm grip on my suitcases, and observe. That was how I found out about Club Eurostar. Officially, it's an Italian railway service that offers members advantages, fast-track tickets, discounts, and a waiting room. In reality, it's a museum of the recent past.

The Club Eurostar waiting room is an astonishing place. I've only ever seen anything like it in stations on the Trans-Siberian Railway. The hall is immense, the ceiling vaulted, the sofas are garish, and the plants ungainly and depressed. Against the left-hand wall is a small, abandoned bar. The staff is busy elsewhere, and the coffee drips, sad and unsupervised, from the espresso machine. At the back, a painting occupies half the wall. A former president of Italy, pipe in mouth, smiles enigmatically between two banknotes.

Club Eurostar! The predictably English name conceals an object from a civilization that some thought extinct, the State-Controlled Age. The United States had a makeover in the 1970s. Japan, Britain, and France invented a new look in the 1980s. Germany followed suit in the 1990s, after reunification. But state-owned Italy has yet to take the plunge. Like an attractive woman of limited means, she has a new coat but is still wearing her old underskirt. Still, there's nothing wrong with that. It's just a little sad, and faintly embarrassing when guests turn up.

●　●　●

I enjoy traveling by rail. Like listening to the radio, or teaching at a university, a train journey lets you get on with something else. I read, browse, write, and put up with people shouting into their cell phones, sharing their most intimate secrets with the entire car, which has no wish to hear them. A few days ago, somewhere between Rome and Bologna, I brushed up on my legal knowledge. A man with a goatee called twenty friends to explain how he had managed to get some trial suspended. Each interlocutor was regaled with new details about lawyers, judges, rulings, and procedural strategies. By the time we reached Florence, I had decided he was guilty.

What do I like about train journeys? I like leaving, to start with. You see a broad sample of humanity toting children and packages, cursing at the weight of their baggage, and smoking along the tracks. Occasionally, someone waves tearfully from a window, as in an old film. I suspect she's an actor hired by the railway company to generate a bit of atmosphere between delays.

I also like the noise trains make. The world of transport may be focusing on soundproofing, but railways continue to make a satisfying din. In a hotel room, the hum of the traffic distracts, the squeaks of the elevator are irritating, and the thrumming of the air conditioner disturbs concentration. But the sound trains make is relaxing. Nothing rattles along like an *accelerato*, which, as we know but you don't, is the slowest kind of train in Italy, despite its name. There is nothing more consoling at the end of a six-hour journey than a voice telling you that you will be arriving ahead of schedule. It's not an announcement; it's an epiphany. Which must be why it happens once a year.

* * *

Italy's trains are places of group confession and collective absolution, which is ideal for a country that calls itself Catholic. Listen to what people are saying. Watch how they gesture. It's performance art. Do you think that confessionals and stages are incompatible? They may be in other countries, but not in Italy.

We are a nation where everyone speaks to everyone else. It wasn't modernity that changed southern Italy's piazzas: the piazzas of the south influenced Italy's modernity. Try to follow the conversations on this train to Naples, via Bologna, Florence, and Rome. They are public exhibitions, with their own rituals, virtuoso touches, unexpected confidences, and surprising fits of shyness. One quickly reaches a note of intimacy in Italy, and speaks about personal matters. Stendhal said that, and he hadn't even been on a Eurostar.

Look at those three. They could be colleagues returning from a business meeting. They're not talking, they're making announcements. They're not communicating, they're issuing mini-bulletins, drafted by the mini–media offices each has in his or her head. As you can hear, they're arguing. And revealing some quite amazing details. They tackle one topic after another, piling arguments—and voices— on top of one another. Actually, the train is the archetypal talk show. It offers a set, a backdrop, personalities, and every station is an opportunity to make your exit.

Here in this car today, we have two business consultants, a superintendent of fine arts, a former hippie who is now the personnel manager of a food company, a DJ, a small businessman, a golfer, a journalist, and a retired manager of a finance company who is carrying out a character assassination of his former boss. The good-looking pharmacist who is reading a book on Iraq has been given the same seat booked by an attractive young blonde. The males present celebrate the mix-up by offering to entertain both.

Listen to the conversations. The choice of words is baroque, a further demonstration of the importance of aesthetics in Italian life.

Do you know why members of Parliament never agree but "register a substantial identity of opinion"? Or why it never rains on the weather forecast but "some precipitation is foreseen following an intensification of cloud cover"? It's because verbal complexity is a form of protection ("I was misunderstood"), a decoration ("See how well educated I am?"), and a declaration of belonging ("I am a member of the caste of doctors, weather forecasters, or lawyers, and I'm sorry but that's how we talk").

Take another look at the trio in the first seats. The attention each devotes to listening to the opinions of the others is misleading. Observe the tense lips and shifting eyes. Silence is the pause that precedes speech. Susan Sontag wrote that during conversations in Scandinavia the physical tension that builds up in the interlocutors is almost palpable ("There's always a danger that the gas will run out, because of the imperative of self-restraint and the attraction exercised by silence"). That's one risk we don't run in Italy, as trains amply demonstrate.

•  •  •

Abroad, they say there's no point in learning Italian. All you need to do is watch the hands. It's not true, but there is insight in the insult. Italian gestures are many and effective. They have intrigued anthropologists, photographers, cartoonists, and linguists. There is even a supplement to Bruno Munari's *Dizionario italiano* that contains only photographs of communicating hands ("Move on," "Come back," "Wait a minute," "What do you want?").

You don't need to classify them, as the Neapolitan canon Andrea de Jorio did in 1832. You just need to understand the verbal concept in the hand movement.

Watch the hands of that squabbling couple over there. Gestures away from the body mean "go away," "get out," "stand back." Down-up gestures say "pay attention," "success," or "resignation." Up-down gestures express disappointment, difficulty, or disapproval. Circular gestures say "move around," either physically or metaphorically. Gestures to the head indicate comprehension, intuition, or idiocy. Gestures to the eyes, ears, nose, mouth, or stomach say "listen," "look," "smell," or "eat." Fingers bunched together indicate combination, complexity, or confusion. Fists express rage or irritation. Open hands indicate willingness to cooperate, or resignation. And so on.

Do you still not understand what those two are talking about? Let's see, now. He's got his fists clenched, so he's angry. She's holding her hands up, palms toward him, which means he should calm down. He's rubbing his thumb and forefinger together, which means "money." She's bringing the forefingers of both hands together, which means "They have an arrangement." So it's easy. They think someone's on the take. Still, I can't expect you to understand all this after just one lesson. You'd need a doctorate, but ten years in Italy would do instead.

*   *   *

Do Italians know how to laugh? I'd say so. Perhaps too much. Giacomo Leopardi, an Italian poet who loved Italians even after he realized who he was dealing with, claimed we make fun of everything because we respect nothing.

There is a grain of truth in that. The Italian character has a skeptical side that borders on cynicism. There is a worldly-wise power of observation running through Italian literature, cinema, theater, and daily life. In the villages, people still have nicknames. These are often cruel but always imaginative, and many Italian surnames also reflect a caustic sincerity. Bassi, Grassi, Malatesta, and Zappalaglio respectively mean "short," "fat," "bad head," and "dig the garlic," revealing a bitter realism. When an Italian laugh arrives, it comes from the belly. A British laugh descends from the brain. An American guffaw comes from the heart and emerges from the mouth. A German laugh starts in the belly and stays there.

Our problem, then, is not laughing. If anything, it's smiling, partly because no one gives us much reason to do so. Public figures with a sense of humor do exist, but they are almost ashamed of the fact. Unless it is solemnized by Woody Allen, or embellished by languages we do not entirely understand, we consider irony to be a form of detachment, and silently disapprove. Inevitably, the Italian witmeister turns nasty. Smiles become guffaws, then fade to sniggers.

This degeneration of irony into sarcasm, and of sarcasm into invective, is worth studying. But we haven't got time, so I'll just pass along a suspicion that is not just mine. Some things in Italy are so grotesque that satire is not only impossible, it's pointless. You no sooner spot a paradox than someone else does something even more absurd. It's no fun, and it's not fair.

## The museum, beautiful women on the walls

Italian museums are astounding. They could put on five years' worth of exhibitions in New York with what Florence's Uffizi has in the basement. But there's a downside to this good fortune. If you have too much on the table, you may lose your appetite. Non-Italians arrive with about ten paintings in their heads—the profile of a duke, the unembarrassed smile of a scantily clad noblewoman and the like—go to see them, and enjoy the experience. We take everything for granted. We've already seen the duke, and the lady has a familiar look.

There's an expression in Italian that sums up this attitude, *roba da museo* (museum fodder). The painter and writer Emilio Tadini said that a painting, an object, a program, an idea, or a proposal could be museum fodder. It had to be "something outside life, buried in the past, that has absolutely nothing to do with us." Why? Perhaps it's a feeling of discomfort. Our forebears were so brilliant we prefer to avoid comparisons. Or perhaps, as I was saying, we are too used to museum fodder. We simmer perennially in beauty, and feel we shouldn't have to buy a ticket to go and see some.

In Italy's parish recreation grounds, ancient frescoes gaze down on the children playing soccer. For us, this is normal. In America, the moms and dads would either be taking photographs, or blacktopping the pitch to turn it into a parking lot. Italy has most of the planet's artistic heritage. Spain comes after us, but has less than you can find in Tuscany alone. But, with a few exceptions, even this no longer excites us. Unless we can make some cash out of it, or impress the rest of the world.

In this case, many of us are moved by self-interest or national pride, and applaud. We have learned to appreciate Italy's national genius in an export format, particularly when it coincides with an event, a special occasion, or a moment we will be able to talk about.

I remember the lines that twisted up the helical ramp of the Guggenheim Museum in Manhattan for the exhibition *The Italian Metamorphosis*. There were Italians waiting to see works that, like us, had crossed the ocean. On show were clothes by Valentino, posters for films by Rossellini, Sottsass's typewriters, Gio Ponti's chairs, and Piero Manzoni's canned excreta. The American museum attracted us as much as the genius of Italy. We realized we were the stars of the show, and were anything but disappointed.

* * *

In contrast, here in Italy, stupendous works of art displayed in modern Europe's oldest museum can look banal, unless we have to defend them in the face of superficial comments. In that case, we— sometimes, not always—manage to see them with other eyes.

Take Botticelli. He's become a stock Italian icon, and we can't let that happen. He was a complex individual, and his work is intriguing.

For a start, he wasn't called Botticelli. His real name was Filipepi. Born the son of a Florentine tanner in 1445, he was apprenticed to a goldsmith, whose name he took. He could paint. As a boy, he frequented the workshops of the artists Filippo Lippi and Andrea del Verrocchio. He read Dante, and knew Leonardo da Vinci, who was seven years younger.

Sandro Filipepi aka Botticelli was a bright, difficult lad, with good connections. His friend and patron was Lorenzo di Pierfrancesco de' Medici, cousin of Lorenzo the Magnificent. He enjoyed being with friends, and had a reputation as an extrovert. Botticelli earned well, but also spent liberally. The story goes that he detested marriage and women. But you wouldn't think so, to judge from his work.

Just look at the *Primavera*, which he painted at the age of thirty-three. On the surface, it is a simple image, an allegory from a classical myth, as was the custom in those days. But the mysterious central figure is fascinating, and experts have identified five hundred species of plant in the scene. Let's admire this *Madonna of the Magnificat,* which Botticelli painted in 1485. A real, beautiful woman without makeup poses among decorative angels. Or the *Calumny of Apelles,* from 1495. The "naked Truth" looks like an actress who has aged before her time, like Florence's political and commercial fortunes after the discovery of America.

You might think this is normal artistic development. I would reply that the artist had sensitive antennae. Botticelli's story is that of a typical Italian and at the same time a reflection of the eternal Italy, the land of insight and transformations. Italy is a country where people's heads are constantly busy. They don't always produce masterpieces. In fact, disasters are frequent. But, in mitigation, we do at least pay for the disasters.

We're there now. This is *The Birth of Venus,* the one with the young goddess in the seashell. Like Leonardo's *Mona Lisa,* it's so famous it runs the risk of looking sentimental. Instead, it's beautiful, wonderful, with its white horses, the trees on the shore, the oval faces, sensuous expressions, and wind-ruffled hair. At that point in his life, Botticelli was striving to reconcile Plato and Christ in a representation of the beauty that derives from the union of spirit and matter. He succeeded. But superficial observers see only the symbol of an unchanging Italy. They see flowers, sea, and a girl surfing on a seashell that would look good on a soap label.

It's a trap. For five hundred years, you've been falling into it, and we've been chuckling as we watch.

*   *   *

Look at the faces in these portraits. They're not from Mars. They're Italians. They are familiar because, as I was saying, we occasionally recognize them. Try to remember them when we leave. You'll see similar faces in the streets and cafés of Florence. As you sip your coffee at the Giubbe Rosse, you might say, "Where did I see her before?"

The answer is, hanging on the walls of the Uffizi, although the Uffizi version wasn't shrieking into an ultra-miniature cell phone.

Genetics is art in Italy. This evening, you'll notice twenty-year-olds from the provinces that resemble Giorgione's *Portrait of a Gentleman in Armor.* Lose the armor, forget he's a gentleman, and you'll see him behind the wheel of a black Volkswagen Golf with his weatherproof face and strong nose, punching numbers into a cell phone as he organizes his evening.

Raphael's Madonnas—the ones that have been gazing down on Italian beds for centuries in endless reproductions—have Italian faces. As you travel round Italy, you'll find women in the Veneto who look like a Mary Magdalene by Giovanni Bellini, Sicilians with the excited smile of Antonello da Messina's *Madonna of the Annunciation,* and Milanese ladies who watch you with all the suspicion of Leonardo's *La Belle Ferronnière.* They are beautiful yet unassuming, and only apparently demure.

The same is true of the countryside. There, too, we see Italy, whether we want to or not. Despite the passage of time, some necessary changes, and other avoidable brutalities, we still see familiar scenes that perturb us but do not repel. We may displace or despoil them, but these are our backdrops.

Take, for example, the *Sacred Allegory* by Giovanni Bellini, also known as Giambellino, one of the most meticulous photographers of the Italy of his day. The landscape behind the figures recalls the spot where the river Adige narrows, near Rivoli Veronese and not far from Lake Garda. It's the proud foyer of our Italian theater, the view that greeted new arrivals as they crossed the mountains. It is a mirage of the Mediterranean. Today the foreigners continue to arrive along the same routes, but few of them stop to look at the river Adige. It's not a great spot for windsurfing.

Observe the dry countryside behind the profiles of Federico da Montefeltro and his wife, Battista Sforza, and the allegorical triumphs on the back of the panels. Piero della Francesca painted Montefeltro as if he were looking at him from a cloud. Nowadays, very few people visit the area. Most prefer the beaches of the Adriatic. But we recognize those barren hills and sparse trees, for they have stuck in a corner of the Italian conscience. They are our full-color regrets. Are anyone else's as lovely?

## Television, where the Semi-Undressed Signorina acquires a cloak of significance

You've heard about Italian television. Now let's watch some. In any case, it's raining, and Florence is swarming with Japanese tour groups in identical raincoats. After all, television is just another Italian museum, with a fine collection of suntans, dyed hair, and fixed smiles delivered at minibar height.

Television in Italy is as exotic as an airport, as unruly as a city street, as hypnotic as a hotel, as perturbing as a store, as ever-changing as a restaurant, as noisy as a train, as deceiving as the countryside, as instructive as a piazza, and as ubiquitous as churches. But if the churches are emptying, television holds on to its faithful. Fifty years ago, people talked about the television of the people. Nowadays, we are the people of the television.

RAI Television broadcast its first program in 1954. It was chaste, instructive television. It didn't tell us what we were like; it told us what we should have been like. Today's Italian television is much more youthful. It's thirty-something, or thereabouts. Actually, it's the daughter of the first private stations in the 1970s, an excellent example of anarchic progress, the kind we find comes naturally. The first private TV station was called Telebiella. I remember TeleAltoMilanese. It paraded a chorus line of reassuringly florid females with generously low necklines and a poor command of Italian grammar. Game show hosts belonged to a new, red-blooded species. I kept expecting them to step out of the screen and ask me for a towel to mop their sweating brows.

In the 1980s, it was the socialists, the most modern and least scrupulous of the period's powerful, who helped Silvio Berlusconi transform this slightly overblown—and therefore very Italian—carnival into an aspiring American-style big business. He didn't invent its taste or its audience. He guessed the former, and pandered to the latter. Did he know that one day the audience would become the hard core of his electorate, doubly precious because it was lifted from the Left? I don't think so. If in 1980, the year Canale 5 was born, Berlusconi had been able to foresee the anticorruption campaign that would sweep away his political protectors, and his own entry into the electoral fray with the big guns of television behind him, he would have been gifted with second sight. Which he isn't. He is a spinner of dreams, skilled at turning reality into entertainment. Without realizing it, Berlusconi took Norman Rockwell's America of lavish dinner tables, smiling old people, and shapely girls, and then imported it, adopted it, adapted it, undressed it, and pretended it was real. Embarrassingly, we fell for it.

●  ●  ●

The new Italian icon is the Semi-Undressed Signorina. We ought to put her on coins and stamps. Her face is interchangeable, but from the neck down everything stays the same. She turns up in every TV program, wiggles her hips, and every so often gets to speak, especially when she has nothing to say.

Realizing that this homegrown siren is the object of Italy's collective desire was a stroke of genius. You can smile at Silvio the politician, if you like, but don't underestimate Berlusconi the adman. He knows what his consumers want before they ask for it. He understood that millions of Italians dream of doing a bit of sinning, repenting sincerely, and then starting all over again. "Guys," he said, "I've got just what you're looking for."

We're not talking about some den of corruption. We're talking about a country that went straight from chronic inhibition to uninterrupted titillation. In Italy, calendars with naked women have emerged from the car-repair shops, where they had a certain dignity of style, and moved into our homes, via the small screen.

Look at this evening's commercials. There are dozens of products advertised through sexual imagery or allusions—aftershave, air conditioning, antitheft devices, apéritifs, automobiles, bananas, beer, biscuits, cell phones, chocolates, chronometers, coffee, deodorants, dishwashing liquid, divans, and duvets. And that's only up to the letter "d."

Radio has fallen into line. If you play your cards right, you don't need pictures to titillate. Management software can be advertised with suggestive sighs and double meanings. A business service is sold as if it were a sex act ("Ladies, bring your friends. I've got something special for them, too!"). One insurance company invites listeners to ring its call center, and hints that you have to say "Ciao, baby," to the operator. Try saying "Ciao, baby," to an American customer-service clerk. You'll find yourself with a sexual-harassment suit or a slap in the face.

Why has sex become the mechanism of choice for advertising in Italy? Simple. Because it sells. When a neckline plunges to meet a hemline, it attracts and entertains the Italian public. If a management-software producer in any other Western country were to present itself to the public with questionable military-type humor (in the army, they'd call it "advertising humor"), potential customers would think, "This is not a serious product. I'll buy something else." But not in Italy. The management software gains notoriety and gets recognized, and people buy it. Competitors take note, and consider following suit.

You might ask why Italian womanhood puts up with all this. The answer is, out of habit, resignation, and a lack of awareness. Thirty years ago, feminists complained if anyone reminded them they were women. Today they watch programs with scantily clad Barbie Doll lookalikes, bemoaning the fact that they can't be like that. Then they are astonished at the glances and offers they get during job interviews. They wonder why the average female salary is 35 percent lower than a man's. They are amazed at the male monopoly of the jobs that count. The percentage of women in Italy's Parliament is the same as Morocco's: we're tied for seventy-ninth in the world table.

If you think about it, their astonishment is quite astonishing.

＊ ＊ ＊

Superstition is widespread in Italy, and takes many forms. It starts with horoscopes, and rituals related to gambling, a passion in which we are outstripped only by Americans, and on which we spend 240 euros a year each. It continues with routine apotropaic gestures, such as throwing salt over the shoulder, avoiding black cats, not walking under ladders, and other I-don't-actually-believe-in-it-but-you-never-know classics. After that comes the moral cowardice of those who fail to protest when they hear someone being called a jinx, an accusation that many Italians still take seriously. The next stage is a religion that some regard as simply a vast collection of good-luck charms. And, finally, there is the cavalcade of fortune-tellers and the like on TV, tolerated because they are looked on as the small businesses of scam.

This is worrying, for we run the risk of losing an Italian privilege.

To date, the country has yet to produce a totally excluded underclass dependent on trash television. There is no slice of Italy that does not vote, does not matter, and does not strive to improve its lot. There is no American-style white trash, a term that in Italy for now refers only to garbage separation.

Classes that are weaker—by reason of lack of education, opportunity, or income—have always behaved with dignity here. They were dignified in postwar Naples, and the Veneto countryside in the 1950s. Lombards behaved with dignity when the factories were in full swing, there was dignity in Piedmont when immigrants were flooding in from the south. Recently, I was tidying up the books in my home, an activity that always leaves one with dirty hands and a guilty conscience. I found a small tome by Pier Paolo Pasolini entitled *Il canto popolare* (*The Popular Song*). This is how it begins:

> *Improvviso il mille novecento*
> *cinquanta due passa sull'Italia:*
> *solo il popolo ne ha un sentimento*
> *vero: mai tolto al tempo, non l'abbaglia*
> *la modernità, benché sempre il più*
> *moderno sia esso, il popolo, spanto*
> *in borghi, in rioni, con gioventù*
> *sempre nuove—nuove al vecchio canto—*
> *a ripetere ingenuo quello che fu.*

> Abruptly, nineteen
> fifty-two passes over Italy.
> Only the people feel it
> truly. Never removed from time, nor dazzled
> by modernity, though always the most

modern, the people, scattered
in hamlets, in neighborhoods, with youth
ever new—new to the old song—
naïvely rehearses what once was.

Then something happened that not even Pasolini could have fore-seen. Television arrived, and there were changes in relationships at work, in the market, in availability, and in political parties. The old communists might have had grotesque political models, but at least they had pride. Today the Left dreams of a world long gone, defends vested interests, and thinks about business. Its leaders argue over who is going to command the troops, but never look round to see if the troops are still there.

Nature, however, abhors a vacuum, especially in politics, and particularly in Italy. We know who filled the vacuum in the last election, but not even Silvio Berlusconi—long an idol of the people "scattered in hamlets, in neighborhoods, with youth ever new"—can stop some Italians from sliding into the embrace of television fortune-tellers.

My impression is that those Italians have no guides, and aren't looking for any. They have no opinions, and don't want them. Their dreams extend no further than next Sunday's soccer game. The sensation I get is that part of Italian society is becoming passive and resigned to enjoying only the trivial consolations of the more than twenty thousand fortune-tellers, the premium-rate telephone chatlines, and the televisual world of recreational grief and artificial euphoria.

It's a shame, because until now Italy has avoided certain social divides, despite our limits and lazinesses. We don't have endemic alcoholism, or epidemics of teenage pregnancies. There are no sports for the poor and sports for the rich, or working-class schools and middle-class schools. Italy is an unruly nation, but uniform in its unruliness. Part of the credit for that goes to television, which is now on the point of tearing down what it helped to build up.

*　*　*

I know that "conflict of interest" is an irritating expression. If you want to lose an Italian friend, or kill off a conversation, all you have to say is "On the subject of conflicts of interest . . ." If your interlocutor hasn't disappeared, he or she will smile condescendingly. Potted plants, if Italian, will start to wilt visibly.

Is Prime Minister Silvio Berlusconi right, then, to say that the issue has been settled by the ballot box? Is he justified in repeating that Italians knew who he was (a media tycoon), and what he owned (a lot), and that when they elected him they showed they didn't care?

No, for two reasons. First of all, he promised to clear up the conflict of interest once he was elected, and didn't. Second, Mr. Berlusconi's awkward position will not be tackled until Italians see it as a problem. Of course, they won't see it as a problem until they are told it is one by television, which is the crux of the conflict of interest. It's what the Americans call a catch-22. But try and explain Yossarian to the Italians, if you can.

We do have a mitigating circumstance. Or two. Well, three, actually.

The first is historic. We've got used to bad habits. The main political parties used to commandeer a channel each, and peddle their own versions of the truth. Over the years, politicians have managed to instill the idea that what is good for them is good for the country, because political parties represent everyone's opinions. It's a false syllogism, and a colossal lie. The truth is that politicians want to see themselves on the evening news.

Our second excuse concerns Italian society, which is awash in conflicts of interest. Banks offer savers their own financial products. Journalists run media agencies. Architects get themselves elected to town planning committees. Teachers give private lessons to their own pupils at state schools. Silvio Berlusconi's conflict of interest is spectacular, but it's not the only one, say some of his supporters. Yet, even if this is true, a head of government ought to set an example, not a precedent.

Finally, Silvio Berlusconi's dominance of television fails to shock us for a historical reason. The only institutions imprinted in Italy's civic DNA are the *Comune* (Municipality) and the *Signoria* (Feudal Lordship). Everything else is imported, parliamentary democracy included. Some of our institutions work well; others not so well. According to Giuseppe Prezzolini, a writer who knew his Italians, our Renaissance forebears thought, "Of course the *Signore* is going to look after his own interests!" Little has changed. Many Italians still think that way, and act in consequence. You're better off flattering the *Signore*, or taking advantage of him, than asking him to act fairly.

# Day Five: In Tuscany

The countryside, where we show that Italians are
the world's leading manufacturers of emotions

The Tuscan countryside is beautiful, but unforgiving. It rejects intimacy. You can paint all the watercolors you like, but it's not a place
for picnics. The blue sky, ocher soil, maternal oaks, and guardian cy-
presses are gentle, bleak, and ubiquitous. See how firm and reassuring the hills are. That's Italy's signature shape, the profile of old
scooters, young breasts, bread on the table, and the classic Lancia
Appia automobile. But note also how dry those lumps of plowed
earth are, and how unforgiving the marble slabs in the courtyards.
Listen to the harsh-sounding nicknames, and the clear, dry speech
of the people. Tuscan is an unambiguous tongue that bristles with
restrained violence. In these parts, polemical debate is a sport for
professionals. Don't be tempted to join in.

Tuscany encapsulates the basic misconception about Italy—the gentleness is prickly, but you prefer not to see the prickles. The American hero in *The Garden of Eden* says, during a vacation in Provence, "We'll turn our back on all the picturesque." Hemingway's resolution is a good one, but it slips people's minds when they come to Italy.

See that name? Bellosguardo (Lovelylook). It enshrines a philosophy, and a marketing strategy founded on crags, bird's-eye views, dark fields, and swimming pools, the only concession to the color blue. How can you fail to like this Italy? It was made to be drooled over. With its lavender, bowers, good olive oil, cool wine, bright eyes, and tingling senses, this is Italian countryside to look at, but not to touch. Tuscany isn't a looming backdrop, like headline-hogging Sicily, nor is it full of stones and mystery, like Sardinia. And it isn't the empty but industrious Po Valley. Tuscany is an ancient, literary setting. It risks being perceived as a sort of Nativity scene, with statuettes of picturesque little Tuscans, busy doing this and that, and visitors, like the three kings, bringing gifts of gold, frankincense, and myrrh. Especially gold, but cash and all major credit cards are also welcome.

Don't be ashamed of your bucolic enthusiasms. Everyone falls victim. In the past few years, people from the rest of Italy have also been flooding into Tuscany. Journalists and their families vie for space with gargantuan machine harvesters. Reconnoitering product managers sniff the night air at their bedroom windows, only to be driven inside by the mosquitoes. It's the unsustainable lightness of sustainable tourism. The environment can sustain it, and so can your wallet, more or less. It remains to be seen what the kids think, having been woken by the farmyard poultry an hour after getting back from the club.

Needless to say, non-Italians are the champs in the naïve-enthusiasm stakes. I brought back from Washington half a dozen Starbucks cups. The series is called *Postcards from Italy*, and each cup sports a watercolor of cypress trees, hills, villas, and pastel façades, as well as a message along these lines:

Dearest Friends,
Everyday the signora hangs our laundry to dry . . . the sweet smell of the clean sheets intoxicates our souls—and makes us ask . . . Why do we ever want to return . . . ? Kisses to you all.

Even that hard-line feminist of yesteryear Germaine Greer talks like a Starbucks cup when she is describing Tuscany. She speaks of "velvet nights spangled with fireflies, dazzling days among fields of mixed grain deep in shady vines and the steely shimmer of olive groves, nightingales flitting from tree to tree by night and turtle doves cooing on the tiles by day." On her first morning, she recalls, "I staggered out on to the *ballatoio* [running balcony—Trans.] into a mother-of-pearl morning" dreaming of "straying amid the fields drunk with dew."

I suppose it could have been the Chianti. In that case, we can forgive her.

•  •  •

Have you seen the walls? Exposed brick as far as the eye can see. The bricks are the same size and color. There are bricks on the churches, bricks on the houses, bricks on the restaurants, and bricks over the entrances. But wasn't Tuscany once a symphony of plaster, composed in local materials to put the colors of the countryside onto the walls? Why has it all been scraped off? I don't know, but I can hazard a guess. You like this earthenware-colored Italy. It's a reproduction of your winter dreams. So should Italy be offering you this? Maybe not, but it is.

Our keenness to please is generating some delightful disasters. Pienza, Montepulciano, Cortona, Casale Marittimo, San Gimignano, and Casole d'Elsa—all the loveliest towns have been diligently peeled. They're trying to keep up in Umbria, at Spoleto, Città della Pieve, and even Assisi. The result is an odd kind of perfection, a nonrustic rustic effect that reminds me of the neo-Tudor style in England, only there it's wooden beams, not brick. At least in England it's a revival. Our version is a fabrication.

Still, removing plaster is not a new idea. It dates back to the nineteenth century's obsession with historicism. Before then, all monuments were plastered and painted. Even stones and marble were stained. Austere Romanesque architecture was covered with a thin layer of plaster, and then painted to look like brick. The ancients couldn't stand the very thing that fascinates us—those subtle differences in the color and finish of exposed brickwork.

Why should we deprive walls of plaster's protection? It's as if we ourselves were to go around in swimwear during winter. When you see yet another brick arch, bobbing like a cork over a plaster façade, you know that Jack the Stripper has been at work. When you enter a yellow-brick *agriturismo* farmstay—they look like housing projects in London, so the British must feel right at home—salute the Plaster Stripper's Apprentice. And when you come across an Undressed Church, think to yourself that the architect who did that is like an Italian cook in New York who puts fettuccine Alfredo on the menu. No Italian is ever going to order it, but Americans expect it, and the customer is always right.

Are there any explanations? Well, there are various reasons of a psychological (inquisitiveness: "Let's see what's under the plaster"), psychoanalytical (stripping a wall is like stripping a lover), or economic (stripping means work means money) nature. But again I would say that we too often agree to adapt Italy's image to the fantasies of our guests. We offer a vast Tuscany of the mind that stretches from Tarvisio down to Trapani. These days, we are the world's leading manufacturers of emotions. Perhaps we should apply for a patent, and bottle them. We could sort out the country's finances in a trice.

* * *

Here in Tuscany, they strip away façades. Elsewhere in Italy, we fence in, which is worse. The countryside is one great enclosure. There are pointless railings, hedges we could live without, inexplicable wire fences, ominous bay-tree barriers, and long walls that look as if they were painted by the futurist artist Mario Sironi.

The Italian countryside has been brutally "anthropized," as people say when they don't want to use the term "battered about." Ours is a recalcitrant land, so we have tried to tame it. And, usually, the first step has been to cut ourselves a private slice.

Sometimes the enclosures look naïve, like the ones around empty fields, but they go to show that as a nation we are skeptical. Often they are a mark of arrogance. Around Italy, there are enclosures that defy heaven to strike them down. Sadly, heaven is merciful, and does nothing. Someone up there must have a soft spot for surveyors and architects. These fences have nothing to do with privacy. The reason these eyesores exist is our—bad—taste for possession.

I am familiar with the people Guido Piovene called "the tenant farmers who live in the Po Valley's mind-numbing sequence of vegetal chambers." I know they can be understanding, farsighted, and even poetic, but not when they are involved in a boundary dispute. In these cases, you see ultra-opinionated individuals who dream in acres, think in furlongs, and will take you to court over yards. These are individuals who in the past raised a wall, watched over an embankment, and cut down a neighbor's tree if they thought it was keeping the sunlight off their crops. From the outside world, they expect challenges and will accept defeats. But in their own little kingdoms, sheltered by rows of poplars or marked off by ditches, they demand order.

In other instances, lack of interest is the motive. The small businessman in the Veneto doesn't care whether his factory building in the fields is pretty to look at. If it's profitable and safe, that's good enough. Gray railings rub shoulders with flower-bedecked gardens, monuments to the determination, and poor aesthetic judgment, of their creators. The area around Treviso is one huge Tucson in a spaghetti sauce. When you see it at night from the air, it's a sea of lights. By day, it teems with people driving big, wide cars along small, narrow roads.

In some cases, particularly in southern Italy, fear of envy is the reason for fences. Squalid frontages hide enchanting gardens, glimpsed through half-open gates. It's bizarre. People who have no compunction about leaving an inordinately expensive car in the street are reluctant to show off their lovely homes. The outer wall is the denial that anticipates the question: "No, I'm not rich, and if I were, it'd be my business."

Who knows what compels us to delimit. It's as if the world were too complicated, and we were trying to set boundaries to make it comprehensible. The British are satisfied with a couple of neighbors to hate from behind a hedge, but we are not. We want a moat, like the ones our ancestors had. Since we can't have one, we erect railings, build a fence, or put up wire mesh. Someone, somewhere, is out to get you. The spikes, the razor wire, and the broken glass hark back to the Gothic corner that is in every Italian brain. You can pay a visit, but you do so at your own risk.

•   •   •

A specter haunts Italy: the marker-pen-colored cottage. There are versions in acid yellow, reflector orange, hospital green, chemical blue, toothpaste azure, and psychedelic scarlet. These synthetic colors have been defacing the countryside for some time.

You turn a corner, find a wall that has you reaching for your dark glasses, and think, "The owner must have ordered the wrong color!" Maybe. That color was selected and paid for. After all, these special titanium- and nickel-based dazzlers cost three times the price of regular paint. But the decision was made on the basis of a two-inch-square sample that had the lady of the house squealing, "That's lovely!" Toothpaste azure slapped over the entire side of the home perturbs. Psychedelic scarlet, a hip-hop version of Italian railway-signal-box red, upsets the digestion. Reflector orange is OK, but only if you're a Dutch soccer star or a visionary Ukrainian politician.

The deed, however, is done. The homeowner has to face facts. When he or she comes home in the evening, the marker-pen cottage will be glowing at the bottom of the street. In winter, the shock is cushioned to some extent. Night comes early, concealing the chromatic chaos, and darkness has always been charitable to town-planning glitches. But in the middle of summer, the sun shines pitilessly down. Swallows will nest elsewhere, the mail carrier will turn up wearing sunglasses, but the owners' penance will be to contemplate the consequences of their chromatic caprice day after day.

*  *  *

After the age of rapid urbanization (1950s), the days of reckless enthusiasm (1960s), a period of anxious alarmism (1970s), one of unfocused optimism (1980s), and another of affectionate concern (1990s), we have achieved a vague sense of awareness. Italy belongs to us, and perhaps we ought to remember that. The birth pains of modernity are not yet over. There are still individuals who flaunt the law and a government that decrees they should be amnestied, but at last things are on the move.

There are national parks, protected areas, and environmental associations committed to defending a particular river or bay. It's a form of sentimental privatization that might turn into a sense of responsibility. "Might," not "will." The way the issue is tackled by public administration, schools, and television is still redolent of rhetoric, and the usual spectacular contradictions. For example, Italy produces less than half the solar energy generated by many Northern European countries. And we've got the sunshine.

The worst enemies of Italy's countryside are no longer ignorance and poverty-driven famine. The main threat is greed, compounded by bad taste. Both have wised up, and now claim to be democratic and popular. As I was saying, governments have granted regular, disastrous amnesties for code violations. Too many local administrations, where the builder is the mayor's friend when he isn't actually the mayor, justify these abominations by saying they have generated employment. You don't know whether they are being shortsighted or cheeky.

This is especially true in the south, but no part of the country is free of such irritating medieval guile. Have you ever heard of Bertoldo? He was a character in sixteenth-century literature, a peasant who posed as a champion of experience over education, and of improvisation over preparation. He is the archetypal Italian who survives on his wits, the triumph of unpunished impudence. Well, Bertoldo is still with us. Now and then, he passes himself off as a city councilor, or the director of something. Almost invariably, he wears a jacket and drives a flashy automobile. He changes region, job, and political party, but not his way of working. Fascinating and a little sad, the modern Bertoldo is just another of Italy's carnival masks.

## The Italian piazza, a tool with more cutting edges than a Swiss-army knife

The piazza is a broad church. It has something for everyone, whether old or young, male or female, rich or poor, local or non-Italian. If you want to understand how it works, start with the simple things. Before you admire the Campo in Siena, let's look at this little piazza. We're in Monte Pitoro, in the municipality of Massarosa, in the province of Lucca. Beneath us and not far away, if out of sight, is the Tyrrhenian Sea. Above is another village, Montigiano, clinging to the hillside like a snail to a stick.

Monte Pitoro hasn't even got a real piazza. It's a gap or pass, the Grand Prix de la Montagne in a cycle race that actually comes to town once a year. A tall yellow building huddles along one side, looking ashamed of itself. Where the road widens, there's the Bar Giusti, the former Communist Party offices, and two competing food stores. One is attached to the Bar Giusti and the other, the one with the yellow sign, is run by a couple called Mariangela and Corrado. In between, cars are parked among the white chairs and yellow umbrellas.

Umberto Eco has said that an "Italian bar is a no man's land and an every man's land, straddling leisure and professional activity." It's an impeccable definition, and one that I would like to propose to Signor Giusti. Like an English club, an Italian bar is a place of long lingerings, yet it's also a place for swift passings-through, like a market in China. It's a place where you can clinch a deal, sort out an evening, start a new working relationship, or end an affair over an espresso. Standing at the bar, usually. Vertical emotions hold no fears for Italians.

The Bar Giusti sells cigarettes, creams, disposable razors, and mosquito-repellent coils. It houses a lottery office and a video-poker corner that once reeked of cheap unfiltered cigarettes and small disappointments. Smoking indoors has been banned now, but the disappointments remain. The countertop is polished aluminum, and the white Sanson ice-cream freezer doubles as a newspaper library. The papers pile up, the most recent also being the warmest, because it is farthest from the freezer. The cones are in a plastic display-case that can be lifted for the purposes of inspection.

You have to start here if you want to understand the piazza. And you'll have to understand the piazza if you want to find out what goes on inside an Italian's head.

* * *

Una famiglia vera e propria non ce l'ho
e la mia casa è piazza Grande,
a chi mi crede prendo amore e amore do, quanto
   ne ho.


A real family I don't have
and my home is Piazza Grande,
from those who believe me I take love, and to
   them I give love, all I have.

This is how Lucio Dalla describes Bologna's Piazza Maggiore, a romantic reception center that the local police probably wouldn't like. In another song, "Le rondini" ("The Swallows"), he admits:

*Vorrei entrare dentro i fili di una radio*
*E volare sopra i tetti delle città*
*Incontrare le espressioni dialettali*
*Mescolarmi con l'odore del caffè*
*Fermarmi sul naso dei vecchi*
*Mentre leggono i giornali . . .*

I'd like to get inside the wires of a radio
And fly over the city roofs
Bump into phrases in dialect
Mingle with the smell of coffee
And linger on the noses of the old men
As they read the newspapers . . .

I don't know whether the noses of elderly Tuscans would support the weight of a singer-songwriter from Bologna, small though he is. But I do know that for many years songwriters have been Italy's best sociologists. Ivano Fossati from Liguria explained the coastline. Piedmont's Paolo Conte showed us the dance halls. Roberto Vecchioni described parking lots in Lombardy. Emilia-born Francesco Guccini described the family home, and Luciano Ligabue, also from Emilia, portrayed the highways. The Roman Francesco De Gregori sang about soccer fields, and Lazio's Lucio Battisti showed the edge of town. Piero Marras described the barracks of the *carabinieri* in Sardinia, and the Sicilian Franco Battiato showed us houses on the coast. The hills round here were described by Renzo Zenobi.

Dalla is the unofficial scholar of the piazza, and in his own way shows us that we couldn't do without it. The piazza was originally an open space in front of a church, a complement to a palazzo, the place where four streets met, or simply what was left after a building was pulled down. An Italian piazza happens. Whenever we have tried to create one from scratch, the results have been indifferent. The finest examples are the result of accretion, and have grown into convention centers, cradles, sanctuaries, shop floors, opportunities, old-folk's homes, catwalks, consulting rooms, places to work or work out, and settings to see or be seen in. To understand a piazza, you have to use it, And you can't be in a hurry. The piazza will tell you all sorts of stories, in its own good time.

● ● ●

The civil and religious versions of the piazza have been facing each other off for a thousand years. In many Italian towns, church and city hall shape up like old adversaries who know they need to keep an eye on each other. In some towns, they stand in the same piazza; elsewhere, in adjoining or nearby squares. Today the bell towers and the civic buildings get on reasonably well, perhaps because they've worked out that the real enemy is somewhere else.

There is a commercial piazza, which has aged well. Only the name sometimes betrays how old it is. Italy is full of squares called Piazza delle Erbe where there are no *erbe* (fruit and vegetables) to be seen. Newsstand, pastry shop, barber, bank, drugstore, bookshop, tobacconist, and bar are the format for Italy's commercial piazza, copied by the world's shopping malls. In an hour, we can grab a newspaper, have a coffee, buy a shirt, order a cake, eye up the talent, get a trim, and watch the evening shadows lengthen. To do all that, an American would need half a day, and have to drive thirty miles.

Do you know why e-commerce is so slow to take off in Italy? Partly it's because we don't trust the postal service or online payments, but it's also because computer shopping robs us of the tactile pleasures of choosing and purchasing. Physical perceptions are also part of the Catholic liturgy, in which the senses support the spirit. In fact, you could say that e-commerce is a Protestant invention—sensible, but unsatisfying.

Then there is a political piazza, the one that has staged comedies and witnessed tragedies: Mussolini's war started in Piazza Venezia in Rome, to end in Milan's Piazzale Loreto. The political piazza is where a few useful meetings are held, as well as lots of pointless ones. It's where significant funerals are celebrated, and where, appallingly, bombs go off (Piazza Fontana in Milan, 1969, and Brescia's Piazza della Loggia, 1974, for example). There are hundreds of Piazza Garibaldis, Piazza Cavours, and Piazza Mazzinis where Garibaldi, Cavour, and Mazzini never set foot. There are dozens of Piazza 25 Apriles, Piazza 20 Settembres, and Piazza 4 Novembres, but don't bother asking the kids on Vespas what happened on those dates (the liberation of Italy in 1945; the union of Rome to Italy in 1870; and the end of the Great War in 1918, respectively).

Then there's the working piazza. It's not very touristy. Provisional, functional, and sweaty, it's interesting but never disinterested. It's busy with arrivals and departures of buses, trips, races, and protest marches. It's booked for concerts. It gets taken over by market stalls, and staked out by students and real estate agents. It's not a pretty piazza, but it is useful. If they take it away from us, we complain.

Next there's a theatrical piazza, where roles alternate. Its users take it in turns to be spectators or actors. One of the most obviously stagelike squares in Italy is Capri's piazzetta. People sit outside four bars—the Gran Caffè, Al Piccolo Bar, the Bar Tiberio, and the Caffè Caso—and watch the world stroll by. When the actors get tired, they sit down and members of the public take their place.

And there's a sexual piazza, where traps are set and appointments made. It's no longer the setting you foreigners imagine it to be, the one Ruth Orkin immortalized with her photo *American Girl in Italy* in 1951. No more are bottoms and bosoms paraded in front of hungry-looking males. The men still eye the women, but with a tad more apprehension. Women today eye them straight back.

There's a social, sentimental piazza, where people get to know one another and meet up again. I don't mean that they stroll in the piazza, which would involve the exercise of will. It's a sort of gravitational pull. Side roads and porticoes lead down to a fountain or a monument, bringing people with them. The social piazza is appreciated by residents, who look to it for routine and reassurance. Out-of-towners also use it as a point of reference. Look how people sit in an Italian piazza: on benches, steps, bicycles, motorbikes, walls, railings, curbstones, and chairs in cafés. We watch life drift by from these theater boxes. Every generation renews its subscription, after first swearing it won't.

Last of all, there's a therapeutic piazza. It's the piazza of rest, observation, and beauty, where "the heart arrives more by virtue of poetry than by virtue of history," as literary critic Carlo Bo wrote. It's the piazza of memory, for those who are leaving, and of welcome, for those arriving. Its therapy is serenity recaptured. One evening in June after the First World War, the French poet Paul Eluard was enraptured by the view of Piazza Maggiore in Bologna from his café table near the Church of San Petronio. He wrote, "I am at peace." Bologna and Italy gave him a gift. Someone ought to tell Lucio Dalla.

* * *

You know this place. Or, rather, you recognize it. It's the main piazza in Siena, the one they call the Campo. Just look at how lovely
emptiness can be. The Campo is a pause in the music of the houses.
Its shell-like shape makes it Italy's slightly irregular belly button.

It wasn't designed on paper. The Campo follows the line of the
palazzos that already stood on the Via Franchigena. Not even its
downward-sloping configuration is an architect's invention, for that
simply mirrors the original inclination, which is the semicircular
head of the Montone Valley. The Campo makes a virtue of necessity, and a spectacle of virtue. That's the eternal Italian dream,
which occasionally comes true.

The Palio Horse Race is held here, but that's an extra. The
Campo is spectacular when the horses are galloping round, and it's
even more instructive when Italians are taking a stroll. Look at the
way they move and greet one another. Their striking naturalness
prompts you to act like them. People come here to see and be seen,
which is why they are happy to return the smiles they expect.

It is not clear how long this daily dose of social antidepressants
can continue. Italy's fourteen thousand historic centers, and their piazzas, are under threat from modernity, which is not an ugly word
but can have ugly consequences.

Everyone knows the signs. First the little drugstores go. Then
the bakeries and fruit vendors leave. Banks open, followed by jewelry stores and boutiques. As the services disappear, the residents
leave with them. And when the residents have gone, the historic
center loses its special atmosphere, a mixture of backyard and back
bedroom. When the offices close, the streets empty and the shutters
come down, as they do in downtowns all over America. This is

worrying. We still think that Siena is a nicer place to be in the evening than Salt Lake City.

* * *

What else can you learn in a piazza? Perhaps that Italians change. Anyone who denies this does so because he or she wants them to stay the way they are. The changes are hardly ever spectacular, though. We are like the hands of a clock. If you stare at them, they don't move; look every so often and you'll realize they do.

For instance, we have a new law that bans smoking indoors in public. Before it came into force, there were protests from those who were unable to admit the truth and passed off their own preferences as universal human rights. You might not believe this, but everything went smoothly. There were no bankruptcies, no smokers going cold turkey at the dinner table, no mega-fines, no squabbles, and—I kid you not—very few transgressors.

Ask anyone here in Siena, or in Milan, or Bologna, or Naples. Bar staff and restaurateurs will tell you that they now breathe more easily at work, and don't go home stinking of cigarette smoke. They'll say that they have almost never had to stop someone from lighting up. And when they did have to, a simple "Please don't smoke" was enough to elicit an apology from the smoker, who went outside to indulge.

We're not talking about Cloud-Cuckoo-Land here. These things happened, and continue to happen, in the republic of Italy. So have we all suddenly become law-abiding citizens? No, it's just that we're not stupid. When a law is sensible—and this one is, whatever anarchists, controversialists, and pseudo–civil-rights activists may say—Italians will accept it. When it is enforced through fines and peer-group pressure, we may even obey it.

The idea that Italians are ungovernable has always appealed to those who don't want to govern us. The myth that Italy is past re-demption suits a lot of people. It saves them the bother of redeem-ing us. Remember that the inevitability of lawlessness is a falsehood. Youngsters in Rome began to wear crash helmets when the author-ities decided to fine them systematically. Kids in Naples won't wear helmets, but it's not because they're from Naples. It's because no one enforces the law.

The same is true of seatbelts. In Modena, most drivers use them, but fewer do so down in Modica. Does this mean that people in Emilia are better citizens than Sicilians? Is there a latitude-related civic determinism? No, it's the environment that defines social be-havior. Swiss, Austrian, and German motorists prove this point. At home, they obey all the rules. But as soon as they hit the *autostrada*, many pedal the metal like fleeing bank robbers, ignoring our 130-kilometer-an-hour speed limit (just over eighty miles an hour). Are they crazy? No, they have simply realized that everyone else drives that fast, so no one's going to stop them. In other words, they adapt to their environment. Chameleons, flatfish, and teenagers have been doing the same thing since time immemorial.

This evening, the piazza before us shows that Italy can change and improve—when it wants to. Survey the scene. The strolling bik-ers are all toting helmets. No one is smoking in the bars. Motorists in the street round the corner are belting up. Was all this predictable five years ago? Not at all. The undisciplined motorist and the arro-gant smoker were givens in Italy, part of a manifest national destiny. No one thought it was possible to bring a little common sense onto the roads or into the bars, or to convince some Italians to leave the car in the garage. Yet the pedestrian Sundays made necessary by traf-fic pollution have been a success. You also need to remember that we are world champions at turning a problem into a party. Since we have a heap of problems, we've got parties lined up for at least a century.

That's not too bad a prospect, if you think about it.

## The window, framing fantasies that are sometimes cut short by a shutter

There are no scholars of the Italian window. Needless to say, architects, surveyors, builders, carpenters, painters, and voyeurs deal with them on a daily basis, but no one gives windows the attention they deserve. Stimulators of our originality, bad taste, imagination, curiosity, conformism, and competitive spirit, windows are orifices that continue to excite the Italian nation.

The country is narrow. Houses crowd together. We argue over—and from—windows the way Americans squabble over their lawns. In 1998, the Canadian Center for Architecture mounted an exhibition called *The American Lawn*. There was a section dealing with litigation over the nation's grassy stretches. In Italy, the civil code's distinctions of "lights," "views," and "prospects" have occasioned equally artistic, and similarly vitriolic, legal actions.

The window is not just the frame for our fantasies. It also testifies to changes in taste and lifestyles. For one thing, the old Italy of roll-up blinds is turning into the land of *vasistas*. Few realize that this sea change is under way.

The blind—*tapparella* in Italian, from the verb *tappare*, to close—turns a room into a pitch-dark catacomb. When lowered, it tells the outside world that communication is not presently desired. If Juliet's room had been fitted with blinds, Romeo would have given up, and Shakespeare would have had to look for another plot.

The classic *tapparella* consisted of a roll of wooden slats, a box over the window, runners, and a cord that would fray and hint at problems to come. Some types were operated with a pull-out handle. When the handle got out of control, it flicked back and forth like a switchblade. The *tapparella* had its own noise. It rose confidently in the morning, and slid down like a guillotine at night, as if released by a halfhearted executioner. Blinds have given way to airtight seals and double glazing, which render them superfluous. For about fifteen years, the only places where new ones have been fitted are hotels and hospitals, but they continue to be a keynote of Italy's townscapes.

The territory abandoned by the *tapparella* has been occupied by other fitments. Shutters are very popular. At the seaside, they often have an Alpine look about them, and vice versa. The classic swing shutter is back, in a range of materials, including aluminum, which gets hot; steel, which costs; plastic, which will fade in the sunlight; and poorly seasoned wood, which warps. Many offices now have floor-to-ceiling glazing, behind which silent staff simmer and wonder whether they have one big window, or no window at all.

The latest fad, as I was saying, is the *vasistas*, a feature that has spread from bathrooms in apartment blocks to detached homes. Many Italians use the term, although few actually know what it means. The name comes from the German *Was ist das?* (What is this?), a humorous name that this turn-tilt window acquired in 1918. Legend has it that it was invented in Italy, which is plausible. The hinge on the lower edge means you can open a *vasistas* while keeping it shut. It's the kind of apparently contradictory operation that would fascinate an Italian.

There have been other functional novelties, such as the apertures that have riddled roofs in Milan since property owners started stretching the interpretation of a new law. Nevertheless, the window is on the defensive. It is no longer the eye on a building's face. Architects and owners are happy if it does its job of illuminating, ventilating, and offering a view. Artistic license is a thing of the past. Gothic two-light windows, lancet-arch apertures, Palladian-style panes, and Baroque ovals have given way to rectangles or squares, or full-length casement windows with a bigger surface area than the garden they overlook. These are offset by windowless bathrooms, a depressing British habit that restructuring has introduced into Italian homes, without thought for the consequences.

Luckily, Italian windows look onto Italy, a privilege that not even the worst builder can remove. Unless, of course, the surrounding landscape is part of the project. It has to be admitted that some have tried, and seem to have had a certain success.

But not here in Siena, thankfully.

•  •  •

The Certosa (Charterhouse) of Pontignano, Palio Room. We're here on the pretext of a meeting, but our real job—one that demands skill and concentration—is looking out the window. You can see that Tuscan Renaissance artists weren't making it up. Your eye sweeps across a painting in the succession of backdrops, the trees that lend rhythm to the distances, and the greens mingling with reds and blues.

The problem is that this ancient beauty conceals the difficult Italy of today. The land you see wasn't combed by a wood nymph. It was churned over by tractors plowing back and forth in the night. They're neither beautiful nor picturesque. No one paints, photographs, or writes novels about them. All they're likely to attract are complaints from people who can't get to sleep.

I told you at the airport when you arrived that your Italy and our Italia are not the same thing. In the past, one or two people have spotted this. Britain's E.R.P. Vincent wrote in 1927: "Italia has a developed sense of her future. Italy has no future, little present, and a preponderance of past. Italia has seasons of cold, dark, dust, and malignant winds. Italy has a fair-weather climate. Italia is a strange, hard land, pulsating and living. Italy is familiar, limited, and defunct."

Well, almost eighty years have passed, and we're not defunct yet. Over the past century, we came close a couple of times, but we're still here. It's another reason not to smother us in overaffectionate stereotypes. Byron said to his friend Thomas Moore, who was gazing over the Grand Canal at the glowing clouds in the west and the fascinating pink shade of Italian sunsets, "Come on, damn it, Tom, don't be poetical." It's still good advice, but not everyone heeds it.

The less celebrated Mr. Vincent did take the hint, as his book, *The Italy of the Italians,* proves. On his journey up and down the peninsula, he seems well aware of the risks of being picturesque. Traveling back up from Naples to Turin by rail, he looks out the window—another window—and wonders, "Can we forget our pretty Italy?"

The answer is still the same: of course we can, but it takes effort. Italy is fascinating, if perturbing. Americans, British, Germans, and Scandinavians gaze on it with rapt suspicion, as if they were staring at a woman who is too good-looking to be true.

The window is one way of establishing distance, but it is still a formidable observation point. Do you remember *A Room with a View*? The title of E. M. Forster's book—and James Ivory's film—confirms that Italy, unlike Britain, which so often takes refuge indoors, and America, which lives in the open air, can be read from a window. The thing is not to become transfixed. Germaine Greer went out onto the porch, and plunged into "a mother-of-pearl morning" to get "drunk with dew." Restrict yourself to admiring the landscape, and shut the window when you've finished.

* * *

Italian windows are never innocent. When they are portrayed—in a painting, a film, or a song—there is a reason. Have you heard of Antonello da Messina? He painted Saint Jerome in his study, and included a slice of Sicily seen through a window in his painting. There's a woman with a dog, two knights, a couple, and a junction of four roads. Italy enjoyed strolling back in the fifteenth century. There were people around to note the fact and tell us about it.

Four centuries later, Giacomo Leopardi wrote "To Silvia" and "Saturday in the Village." He was indoors. Outside, a girl was singing and the village was having a good time. Music, whistles, laughter, and playful cries flood in through the window, which is transformed into a sort of safety valve. Leopardi could see this, although it didn't occur to others: Italy's sound track—in a land that is rarely too hot or too cold—is piped in through the country's windows. Notoriously, we are unenthusiastic abour air conditioning. It upsets our stomachs and discourages poetry.

An Italian window is hardly ever a blank space. It's an opportunity. Ferzan Ozpetek's *Facing Windows* recounts the dreams of two neighbors in Rome. A songwriter from Naples, Edoardo Bennato, wrote "Affacciati, affacciati" ("Come to the Window") and "Finestre" ("Windows"). The first is an invitation, the second a sociological essay. A Polish pope chose a window in Rome as the setting for his farewell to the world.

Lots of Italians like to look out the window, especially in summer. It's not a waste of time, nor is it morbid curiosity. The window is a way of keeping an eye on the territory—they call it "neighborhood watch" in America—and a lifestyle. The British may sit on a fence, and the Chinese—if we want to believe stereotypes—wait on a riverbank. We wait at the window, because it is an instructive platform, and provides entertainment that has only recently been packaged as reality shows.

Dates, engagements, meetings, partings, weddings, funerals, comedies, tragedies, expectations, disappointments, the mysteries of passing, and the consolation of recurrence are all there. As in a reality show, anything can happen before an Italian window, with one difference. The participants throw themselves into the action as if the show actually were real.

# Day Six: In Rome

### The bank, a confrontation of confidence and cold feet

In Prati, there aren't any "meadows," which is what *prati* means. The district's ramrod-straight streets and tall houses between the Tiber and the Vatican take up very little space in the guidebooks, but it is fascinating, as Rome always is when it agrees to act normally. Thirty-four centuries of uninterrupted urban history are enough to crush anyone's spirit, but not the spirit of that girl parking her Vespa. She takes off her helmet, and has a quick glance in the mirror to check that her hair has survived the procedure.

It's noon on Wednesday, and the midpoint of the workweek. At the entrance to this bank there's a liquid-crystal monitor touting investment options—somewhat timidly, as if it knew that recently Italians have little faith in such things, and the Romans even less.

Ubiquitous brochures ambiguously insinuate, "The more we talk, the more we benefit." "What about us?" you feel like asking. A television with the latest stock prices sparkles like a fishless aquarium. The floor is gray linoleum. It looks dirty even when it's not, but it also has the advantage of looking clean when it's dirty. There are bank-green swivel chairs, and prints on the walls. Three sad-looking thirty-year-olds entertain chatty fifty-somethings from behind their desks.

People don't feel under observation in here, and behave naturally. Just look at how they wait. In the rest of Europe, people tend to stand in straight lines. Here we favor more artistic configurations, such as waves, parabolas, herringbone patterns, hordes, groups, and clusters. Our choreography complicates waiting, but brightens our lives. A Briton on his or her own is a queue waiting to form. These Italians, who look as if they are waiting in an orderly fashion, are actually an equivalent number of nascent lines, each with its own direction and intentions.

Few resign themselves to waiting passively. Almost everyone tries to get things moving. One may criticize the bank's organization. Another might gauge how long there is to wait from the number and appearance of the people in the line. For example, anyone depositing cash or checks should have filled in the form beforehand, or time will be wasted at the counter. People wearing eyeglasses are slower, younger customers might not know the ropes, and anyone with a bag arouses suspicion. Inside, there could be piles of checks, or bags of coins.

There aren't so many who try to jump the line nowadays. It's considered too obvious. But there are experts who sneak into already formed lines with childish excuses ("I only want to ask a question!") and know every detail of the local terrain, including side doors, corridors, columns, and openings. Look behind you, and there they are. Look up, and they're next to you. Look again, and they're a couple of yards ahead of you.

Finally, admire this jewel of the popular imagination. The lines don't correspond to the tellers. People are waiting between the windows. Because, that way, people can kid themselves that they are in front of two tellers, and hope to slip across to the line that's moving faster. Is that odd? Of course it is. But this is an Italian bank. Don't be surprised if it surprises you.

     &bull;  &bull;  &bull;

Some objects are emblematic. They have become mental spaces in their own right, and deserve a guided tour. It is not enough to use them. You need to fix your gaze on their horizons, and impress them on your mind. In Italy, one of those objects is the television set, which we talked about in Florence. Another instructive space is the automobile, which we'll be examining. But the grandest, most luxurious space of all in modern Italy is the cell phone.

It's known as the *telefonino*, and in Italy, the diminutive suffix *-ino* is always a bad sign. Watch out if you are asked for an *attimino*, or "moment of your time," a *piacerino*, a "small favor," or a *bacino*, a "little kiss." In recent years, though, the *telefonino* has changed our lives. It has had a greater impact than Silvio Berlusconi, the euro, or *Grande Fratello*, our version of the *Big Brother* reality show. The relationship between cell phones and Italians has spilled over from statistics into our lifestyle. If the French or Germans were to shut their eyes and think of Italy, they wouldn't see the Colosseum. They'd see a guy talking to himself in the street with one hand over his ear. Like that one over there. Observe how he tells the world about his love life as he waits to tell the bank teller about his cash-flow problems.

The guy over there is a video-camera fanatic. Having used his cell phone to hold superfluous conversations, he now uses a camera phone to take pointless pictures. That gentleman over there is a man who discovered texting at the age of fifty. He texts every word in full, with capital letters, accents, apostrophes, and all the proper spaces. Just watch him tapping out a message, his tongue sticking out of his mouth. Other customers avoid him. One or two sneak in front of him, but he doesn't seem to mind. He's trying to find the exclamation point, but has forgotten which button to press.

The astonishing popularity of cell phones in Italy is not due simply to convenience. The new toy also ticks a whole series of boxes in the national character.

The phenomenon started out as a way of showing off ("I've got one, what about you?"). Then cell phones became a token of belonging ("Have you got one?" "Me, too!"). Finally, they were viewed as a necessity ("We've all got one. Couldn't live without them!").

Today's success hinges on the tentacular nature of the Italian family. The Finns own proportionately more cell phones than we do. They'd be very happy to use them all the time, but they don't know who to call. We Italians know only too well. Pop calls Mom, Mom calls son, son calls friend, friend calls other friend from the office, other friend calls casual acquaintance, casual acquaintance calls girlfriend, girlfriend calls sister, sister calls her folks, folks ring uncle and aunt, uncle and aunt call nephews and nieces, nephews and nieces ring home, Mom answers, and then calls Pop, who is standing in line at the bank. The circle is complete. They can start again.

●  ●  ●

Consider this teller. His window is a confessional. That's the secret weapon of traditional banks against Internet banking. For customers, a weekly hello is personalized service. The teller in his cubicle has a name, a receding hairline, and a family. This is reassuring, even in a big city like Rome. Such complicity often leads to embarrassment when, for example, an honest clerk has to justify ridiculously high commissions. It can bring serious trouble—over bond purchases, among other things. But many customers regard the relationship as indispensable. Computers are intimidating. Most don't talk, to begin with, and the ones that can don't have a receding hairline.

I've already told you about the Italian love of personalized treatment. The bank is a good example, but it's not the only one. There's a young man with a bandaged foot. He twisted his ankle playing soccer, he is saying. Before going to hospital, he rang a friend and asked her if she knew anyone in the orthopedic ward. Is he just another line jumper trying to get round the waiting list? No, he wasn't asking his friend for special treatment. He simply thought that if he knew someone in the orthopedic ward, the twisted ankle would be a more marginal, easily managed affair: "in the family," as it were. By knowing someone, even a friend of a friend, no matter if it's a doctor or a nurse, the patient feels he is a special case. One of the fifty-eight million special cases that live in Italy, each proud of his or her uniqueness.

●  ●  ●

Few things reveal national character like money. Cash provides material for psychologists, sociologists, fishers of souls, managers of estates, linguists, statisticians, economists, tax specialists, and tourists. Money is a distillate of sentiments and attitudes, from honesty to shame, sincerity, superstition, prudence, and fatalism.

By and large, we Italians love talking about money. Provided it's somebody else's. When it comes to putting a figure to our own incomes and wealth, we are less liberal with information. Half a million families in Italy have at least half a million euros apiece. And chances are that the lady in front of us, the one with the demure walk, long hair, flat bag, and fashionably pointed shoes, belongs to one such family. There are quite a few of these: one in forty-eight families, in fact.

So why all the embarrassment? Well, there are eternal reasons and contingent ones.

The former include conscience and the tax authorities. The Italian conscience, unsoothed by Calvin, is convinced that money is fundamentally bad. This is not a form of Marxism; it's a neurosis. For many of my fellow citizens, money is the fruit of some mysterious sin. The belief that we have given something good to someone else—a product, a service, or an idea—is mingled with fear. Horror of horrors! People might find out we were paid well. Many of us associate this embarrassment with a sort of Catholic vow of poverty. Money is seen as the devil's ordure. But Catholics have by now realized that money is not, in itself, evil. It is a means with which one can accomplish good things or not-so-good things, do significant deeds or irrelevant ones, and acquire life's necessities or its superfluities. Recently, the latter have been enjoying a certain popularity.

The second reason we do not like to talk about money is that we are afraid someone might be listening. We fear fate, which should not be tempted. We fear others, who should not be provoked. And we fear the tax authorities, especially when we declare ridiculously low incomes. So, when we talk about money, the same golden rule holds true: speak softly, deal in cash, and err on the side of caution.

Our national reticence on tax matters is notorious. Many believe that whispering your income in a bar attracts more attention than double parking your SUV outside. Duty, habit, and apprehension, the sentiments that prompt the rest of the world to pay their taxes, just don't work in Italy. Americans are honest because the cost of tax evasion is very high: fines, prison, and exclusion from polite society. If I declared a laughably low income in the United States, my son would be ashamed of me, and people would point us out in the street. If I did the same thing in Italy, two neighbors would come round to ask me how I did it, and two more would loathe me in silence. No one would report me.

But there's more. We Italians evade taxes because we find a moral justification to do so. The state helps, of course, with its baroque fiscal regulations and crushing tax pressure. The ill-intentioned taxpayer has a whole arsenal of excuses, including the waste of public money, the jungle of privileges, and the bad example set by many of the self-employed. With all this evidence at hand, the tax evader conducts his or her own defense, assisted by the accountant and the bank, which supply regulatory, practical, and psychological support.

Do you remember what I was telling you at that red light? We Italians like to decide when the general rule is applicable to our specific case. The same is true for taxes. We are our own tax authorities, and almost always magnanimously decide not to collect.

•  •  •

There is the History of Italy, with a capital "H," at least from the point of view of spelling. And there is Italian history, with a lower-case "h," which is full of extraordinary episodes. It is our collective past, and in it we have given free rein to all the imagination, realism, and irresponsibility of which we are capable.

If you want to understand Italy, don't overlook the minor phenomena. Take the "minichecks" that invaded the country in the

1970s, when there were not enough coins. They hold more truth than many official speeches. Issued by the banks to make up for a shortage of coins—another exquisite absurdity—the checks were for very small amounts, such as fifty, one hundred, or two hundred lire.

It's of no importance who invented them, who first decided they were collectible, who made money out of them, or who lost it. The minichecks embody several Italian characteristics. They represent flexibility, imagination, taste in graphic design, a love of collecting, conformist individualism, and an all-consuming, if transient, passion. Our ancient spirit of initiative emerged in an entirely new manifestation, a homemade mint. Bankers, bank clerks, and babies all had great fun.

Another milestone in Italy's economic history was the introduction of the ATM in the early 1980s. The Italian name, Bancomat, was supposed to evoke the automation of banking services, but in the early days it could well have meant *la banca mi fa matto* (the bank is driving me crazy).

There were very few ATMs, and most were skillfully camouflaged. The card came with a little handbook that listed the "Bancomats present on Italian territory," and served the same purpose as the map you get for a treasure hunt. Every night, all over Italy, desperate bands of cashless citizens scoured the streets in search of the only ATM in town. Often when they found it they would discover that it was out of order. The ATM PIN code was the first in a long series of crucial personal numbers for faxes, combinations, and so on. It introduced into the Italian language one of those half-official, half-ridiculous phrases that insinuate themselves into the national consciousness, triggering a reflex reaction of atypical obedience. "Enter your secret code, making sure that no one can see." Amazingly, that's exactly what we do, glancing over our shoulders like conspirators.

Ten years later, it was the turn of credit cards. They had existed earlier, but in the early 1990s they became a mass phenomenon. Relatively so, of course. In Italy, plastic money has never enjoyed the success it has known in Northern Europe and the United States. Perhaps it never will. Yet again, it goes against one or two Italian quirks. There is our distrust of anything automatic. Our fear of getting into debt. Our dislike of credit. Our animal unease at leaving any trace of our passage. And the initial hostility of storekeepers and restaurateurs. Even today, many traders prefer payment in cash, which enables them to deny there was any transaction in the first place, a genuine pleasure for a philosophical people.

## The office, the opera house of orderly anarchy

People say we Italians don't work very hard. I wish it were true, because it would mean that we work well. In fact, Italy is an agitated anthill. Three Italians in ten say they work forty to fifty hours a week. Many claim more. In Northern Europe, people work twenty-five to forty hours. At five o'clock, London offices look like a cattery after someone fired a gunshot. There's no one there. Contrast that with this office in Rome. There are plenty of signs of escape, in the form of exotic screensavers, erotic calendars, postcards of palm trees, and photos of progeny. But no one actually leaves.

An office in Italy is a sanctuary of contradictions. Almost all of us put meticulous care and exaggerated passion into our jobs. According to one study, seven Italians in ten complain about their jobs, but worry about office problems in their free time. It's as if we wanted to turn the stereotype of Latin laziness on its head. To do so, we work longer hours, wear a pained look, and adopt a self-mortifying lifestyle in which everyone controls and consoles everyone else.

* * *

What do we enjoy about the claustrophobic rituals of the office? Let's see, now. Above all, we like our colleagues, but not to consult them. We like to scrutinize them. The water fountain is the think tank of the American office. The pub is the decompression chamber of offices in Britain. And the coffee machine is the central intelligence agency of any Italian business. In fact, there is even a very successful television series—*Camera Café*—set around this indispensable device. I once heard of a company near Bergamo that forbids its employees from going for a coffee in twos because it's too risky.

We like to see people's outfits/haircuts/makeup, partly because there's something new every day. The sad conformism of Italian youth—who all have the same backpacks, sweatshirts, and footwear—is replaced in adulthood by a sophisticated exhibitionism. Look around. You won't see the predictable shirts and ties of Britain, or America's ubiquitous sexed-down skirts, high heels, and running shoes tucked under the desk. You will note a constant stream of colors and personal touches, from fragrances to fripperies. When it comes to personal appearance, Italians apply without knowing it the Boy Scout injunction to "do your best."

Every potential asset, from expressive eyes to a generous head of hair or slim legs, is methodically exploited, and compliments on the results are appreciated. If a good-looking American came to work here in a miniskirt, and claimed compensation for the standard local ration of comments, she'd be a rich woman in no time. Of course, every so often someone takes things too far. But comments are almost always peer-to-peer, reciprocal, and welcome.

Italian offices are not metaphorically next door to the bedroom, as many foreigners imagine. Let's say that offices, like many other settings in Italy, are places where people don't just look at you. They *see* you.

•  •  •

Italians like the established order of the office. This is especially true when we are at the top of the heap, but also obtains when we are at the bottom. It enables us to exercise our prudence and intuition. The speed with which Italians manage to read a new space is stunning. After a month, we're at home. After a year, we're veterans; and after three, we consider ourselves to be old soldiers. That's another reason why it's difficult to give us orders. Sometimes we have an inflated idea of our role, and an idiosyncratic attitude toward authority.

Bosses in Italy are no worse than elsewhere. Often they have an excellent relationship with their subordinates. So what's the problem? Some subordinates mistake friendliness for complicity. They say things they shouldn't, and ask for things that are inappropriate. Bosses, on the other hand, tend toward paternalism. If they could, they would select their secretaries' paramours. Since they can't, they make comments on how the secretaries dress for the first date.

•  •  •

One thing we like about offices is meetings, even if they do waste time.

We have all experienced the existential ennui of certain business gatherings. The corporate motormouth gets into gear, and we doodle. The boss summarizes, but we already know the situation, partly because we drafted the summary. The expert gives chapter and verse on X, but we deal with Y. Meantime, the hours drag by, and the light changes on the roofs beyond the windows. The afternoon is over, and we have achieved little or nothing.

Yet some of us—you can read it in the faces—are content. When conscience, in the person of our significant other, asks, "What did you do today?" we'll be able to say, shamming exhaustion and secretly congratulating ourselves, "Today? A whole bunch of meetings." I admit it sounds good. But meetings ought to be a swift means. If they become an end, as they increasingly often are in Italy, then disaster looms.

Once, when I called someone at work and was told, "She's in a meeting," I would think it was an excuse for not putting me through. Now I know that the individual concerned really is in a meeting. And that's serious, at least for the person I'm calling. One of the rules of the modern market economy is this: your status in the company is proportionate to your ability to avoid meetings. Hence "always in a meeting" means "at the bottom of the heap." "Never in meetings" means "top dog."

Every so often, someone tries to break the mold. This individual arrives in the office in a truculent mood, stares the secretary straight in the eye (if the secretary is a woman, she wonders if her mascara has run), opens the diary, and begins to cancel meetings or postpone them sine die. He or she then goes out into the corridor with a satisfied air and says, "Great. So what do I do now?"

•  •  •

Another thing we like about offices is their faint air of absurdity. Every workplace has at least one likable sociopath. Look around. There's bound to be someone in here who does the oddest things with the straightest of faces, making life very difficult for everyone else. Here, as in every other office, there will be a Pink Panther of the liquid soap, a Professor Moriarty of the stationery cupboard, a Butch Cassidy of the tea bags (because the espresso-machine coffee pods don't work on home coffeemakers), a veritable Sundance Kid of the sugar sachets. A thief? A kleptomaniac? Destitute? No, the resident Italian company-property liberator is a man (rarely a woman) who loves challenges. So the boss locked the toilet paper in a cupboard? I'm going to lift it: I can use it in my garage. You keep a close eye on the paper tissues? Well, I'll steal the marker pens, pencils, and sugar. The liquid-soap dispenser is sealed? I can get round that, and it's just as well I'm not a Hindu deity with ten hands to wash.

Since we're talking about office crime, the Italian Court of Cassation, the supreme court, has laid down that anyone who phones home from the office is guilty of an offense. The same holds true for people who chatter too much, do shopping in office hours, or get in some shut-eye, which the court calls "malicious abandonment of the workplace." I say that's great. But now we have to take the next step. Instead of trying to punish billions of crimes and millions of criminals, let's just stick Italy behind bars. It'd be much quicker. Perhaps we can start ordering the fencing. We'll need 7,456 kilometers (4,633 miles) of it, islands included.

* * *

We like the security of offices. For years, open-ended contracts were sacrosanct, but I fear they may be turning into a dead weight. Companies dislike them, and go to amazing lengths to avoid issuing them. They offer training contracts, project-specific contracts, no contracts, apprenticeships, and probationary periods. If things go on like this, we'll have to change the first article of the constitution. It will no longer read, "Italy is a democratic republic founded on work," but "Italy is a democratic republic founded on work experience."

Some companies keep their options open by making newly hired employees sign an undated letter of resignation. For many years, others avoided regular hirings by using "coordinated and continuative collaborators," or "co.co.co." workers on nonstandard contracts. The abbreviation echoes perfectly the clucking of the chicken run into which we have shut ourselves. Now there are project-specific employment contracts, and it has to be said a project does exist: to avoid hiring any full-time staff at all.

Most Italians think a job with an open-ended contract is the only universally accepted collateral—by a partner before getting married, by a bank before it gives you a mortgage, by parents before they'll finally let go, and by your own self-esteem. Those who obtain such a contract, however, find out that it comes at a price. In almost every case, employees' salaries are lower than the earnings of the self-employed, and taxes are higher.

The deal seems to be: "You won't have much money, but you'll have it forever." Companies worry about the "forever," their employees complain about the "not much." And so we go on merrily squabbling over adverbs.

•  •  •

We love the routine of offices. Look around and breathe in the atmosphere. A place like this is a mild intoxicant. Many writers have described the curious consolations of the Italian office worker: novelists (Italo Svevo, *Una vita* [*A Life*]), screenplay writers (Vincenzo Cerami, *Un borghese piccolo piccolo* [*An Average Little Man*]), and humorists (Paolo Villaggio, *Fantozzi*). A retired manager doesn't miss just his power and salary. He mourns the passing of neatly ordered paperclips, his colleagues' respectful greetings, and the noise of his secretary bustling around in the office next door. The secretary will miss the boss's little manias, the tone of his voice on the intercom, and the clock on the wall that counts every second.

It's one of the reasons why telecommuting has never taken off in Italy. Telecommuting accounts for 10 percent of employment in Denmark, for 9 percent in Holland, and for 6 percent in Ireland. Here in Italy, we're stuck on 0.2 percent. It's a pity, because tele-working looks tailor-made for a long, narrow, overcrowded country with inadequate public transport.

Is it the fault of companies and offices that insist on having everything under control? Partly. For some bosses, knowing where the accounts clerk is midafternoon is a source of sadistic pleasure. But subordinates seem to like this sort of gentle bullying. For many people, telecommuting is more like solitary confinement. No more chatting, no more deadlines and lifelines, and no more trivial privi-leges. You might think, "How could anyone actually get to like that sort of thing?" It's possible. Even jailbirds manage to, and they don't just put in eight hours at a time.

●  ●  ●

One of the good things about America is this: failure is not a mark of infamy. After all, to fail you must have tried. In Italy, failure—whether it's bankruptcy, dismissal, or whatever—scars your life. That's something else you should consider if you want to under-stand the allure of an Italian office.

If only you knew how many people never struck out at all for fear of making a false start. If you tell an American you've spent twenty years in the same job, you won't get praised for your loyalty. Eyebrows will be raised. A career move is a good thing, and a career isn't restricted to just one profession. In Italy, we still think in more literal, vaguely cynical terms, that a career move is a move made to advance a career. The nation that, according to journalist Leo Longanesi, wanted to rebel against authority with a permit from the police has grown up but not changed. Few want to take all-or-nothing risks. We dream of risking a little to win everything.

Italians who dare often have something in reserve—a parachute, a spare wheel, another option, or a relative. The ones who start a new job don't leave the old one. In fact, public administration is full of people like that. And people who proclaim that they want a life change do so only when they have no choice, such as TV stars whose contracts have not been renewed. Rudyard Kipling, who admired you if you had the courage to "make one heap of all your winnings / And risk it on one turn of pitch-and-toss," would be mystified if he came back to this world in Italy. We want very much to win, but we are even more afraid of losing. So we settle for a draw.

It's a shame, because people in Italy have the makings of risk-takers. Italian success stories are tales of courage and individual initiative. Take Ferrari. The fastest, most beautiful automobiles in the world come from a small factory in the flatlands of Emilia. Take the entrepreneurs and the businesspeople, the voluntary workers and missionaries, the scientists who have left for America, and the soccer players who have set out for London. None were afraid of making a false start. They were all reasonably irresponsible.

Without irresponsibility, we wouldn't fall in love, or have children. We wouldn't pursue a vocation or an insight. We wouldn't wake up one morning ready to cross the planet or the town. Italy would become a nation living on its investment income and memories. Some say it already is, but I don't believe them. I see it as a Ferrari on the starting grid, its engine throbbing. But it's been there for a while now, and the race is already on the third lap.

The shopping mall, a taste of America
delivered to your door

The names are English—*shopping center, outlet, multiplex*—and the sets are American. Look at those vast parking lots, lines of shopping carts, artificial palm trees, fake streetlamps, tiles, special offers, and ordinary faces.

But the people are still Italian. In the malls around Washington, no one hollers "Maaariooooo!" to attract the attention of a boyfriend on the floor below. But here, in a shopping center just outside Rome, they will do that, and worse. A thousand years of piazza living have left their mark.

America's malls are frequented by men and women with a sense of duty. They have a duty to purchase, a duty to save, a duty to catch the sales, and a duty to select the right coupon. In Italy, shopping malls are full of people having a good time.

Look at the way the families split up, the way they do in airports. Each has an objective to achieve, a purchase to make, or a store to see. This temporary diaspora is productive. When they meet up again, everyone is happy to show off his or her loot, and comment on everyone else's.

See how the young people reproduce the rituals of the town center, the *struscio* (stroll), the glances, the smiles, the giggles, and the huddles. They're concentrated, as if they are looking for something. "Hey there, hunk! Gonna get me an ice cream?" shouts the preteen flashing her navel. The hunk scurries off to do her bidding.

Note the methodical fashion in which the security guards hit on the shop clerks; the friends who call one another on their cell phones to find they're only ten yards apart; the women who stop off at the salon more to exercise their tongues than to get their hair done.

Observe the elderly waiting on the benches. The minister of health proposed bringing them here in the summer, to help them cope with the torrid heat. They'd certainly be cooler here than in the park, and they'd have more stimulation. Pigeons don't wiggle their backsides quite like that, nor do they wear low-slung jeans that show the tops of their underwear.

• • •

Inside a mall, there's always an *ipermercato,* a *grande magazzino,* a *supermercato,* a *supermarket, superstore, discount,* or *cash & carry.* Don't be put off by names in Italy. They're one of the ways we decorate our lives. And never take a place for granted. An Italian *ipermercato* is not just a perfect blend of predictability and the unexpected. It is much more. It's an educational jungle.

Strange creatures lurk among the displays, speaking in outlandish tongues ("Is it two for three?" "Let's buy eight, then"). Mysterious noises filter through from somewhere in the distance. Thumps follow rustlings; falling objects echo slithering ones. Cold (cabinet) alternates with warm (bakery). Dazzling colors surprise at every step. White light blazes overhead, but it is hard to find your way through these walls of color. You feel vulnerable and alone. In a tropical forest, you might meet Tarzan. Here in an Italian hypermarket, you might not even see anyone stacking shelves.

It's a world where I buy things I don't want, want things I can't find, and find things I'm not going to buy. I see products with Baby Oil, Maxi Foam, Moss and Fern, Pine and Cinnamon, Magnolia and Myrrh, or Beta-Carotene and Antibacterial Lily of the Valley. I chase air-conditioned nostalgia in descriptions like Rustic, Traditional,

Farmhouse, and Granny's Own. I yearn for pathetic factory-made reassurances such as Green, Authentic, Organic, and Natural. I am amazed at customer loyalty to certain brands of pasta, peas, cookies, and canned tomatoes. Why? Conservatism, consolation, and television, the same combination that explains certain long Italian careers.

A hypermarket shows how tastes evolve. Bread arrives in a hundred different disguises. Cheeses have become exotic. Salads are now shapely. Fruit is much better looking but has lost its savor, further evidence of the importance of aesthetics. Barbera and Chianti have yielded shelf space—reluctantly, I imagine—to Chilean Chardonnay. The variety in each product is no different from in an American supermarket. In both, there are endless, pointless combinations of taste, color, size, and name.

But all this arrived in Italy at the same time. In the U.S.A., people drank orange juice for breakfast for decades, and then they began to consider a wider range of options. Here orange juice achieved popularity when, and perhaps because, it was available in red, yellow, or orange Sicilian, Portuguese, Spanish, and Israeli versions, with vitamins or carrots, in bottles or cartons.

Many Italians feel overwhelmed. They come home from trips to the hypermarket burdened with useless purchases and heavy consciences. Our ATM card is our passport, and the checkout is Customs, where we pause in apprehension. The checkout girl's apron is a uniform, and I've already said we don't trust uniforms. Our fears soon disappear as our gaze alights on the marvelous products that large-scale distribution places at this strategic point. How can you resist a three- or four-blade razor, even if you only have one face? Why should you deny yourself ballpoints, batteries, or bubblegum?

In America, gossip magazines are sold at the checkout, because customers are dazed by the time they get there and will buy anything. We're catching up over here. If they put a bar code on the checkout lady, we'll buy her, too. She'll also be better value than the other stuff. When you get her home, she can tell you all about what passed by her tree in the surreal jungle of an Italian hypermarket.

* * *

See how people study the prices. The short- and long-sighted are divided by their lenses, but united in their prudence. How many are still nostalgic about the lira, do you think? Not very many, even though the arrival of the euro brought with it some audacious price hikes. Our farewell to the old money in 2002 took place without tears. I've seen more emotion at goodbyes to old cars, old homes, old holiday apartments, and even old marriages.

Why don't our eyes mist over when we think about our old currency? Well, we never really loved the lira. We used it, which is different. The lira never had the personality of the dollar, mark, or franc, which you could actually use to buy something. For more than half a century, one lira was a theoretical concept. To amount to anything, the lira had to be in a group, like sardines or schoolgirls. The monetary unit we do miss is a nice round number, the million.

The euro has another advantage. It is redolent of Europe, and we've always liked Europe. Some say our love for Europe is irrational, and impossible to explain. Wrong. An explanation will be helpful, albeit complicated. A historian, an economist, and a sociologist wouldn't be enough. We'd need a comedian, a marriage consultant, and a fortune-teller.

Now, then, Italians love Europe. We desire Europe in all its manifestations, shapes, and colors, from the maroon passport to the single market, university-student exchanges, and our cell phone ringing on the Champs-Elysées. For the euro, we behaved like young suitors in a hurry to get married. We didn't stop to think, "Can we afford her?" or "What will living with her be like?" We wanted to rush to the altar and the bedroom, in the conviction—shared by fifty-eight million Italians and four Beatles—that all you need is love.

No other European nation behaves like us. Take the British. First they reflect on the inevitable costs and possible advantages of the marriage. Then they look for a home. After that, they sign a mortgage. Finally, they start making plans. If they are not entirely convinced, they postpone the wedding, as they have done with the single currency. Which is the wiser attitude? The marriage consultant—here she comes—will say that the Italians are too emotional, and the British aren't emotional enough.

Italy's carefree, optimistic romanticism is not restricted to ordinary citizens. Our "leaders," for want of a better word, are just like us. Almost all of them prefer brilliant declarations to unostentatious planning. They like first nights but not rehearsals, and want to be onstage rather than behind the scenes. Like us, they behave like agitated Romeos who rush to Juliet's balcony, forgetting the ladder.

From the outset, Italy's European adventure has been scarred by this ambivalence. We sent our best team into the field to prepare the signature of the treaty that founded the European Economic Community in 1957. Once we were in, we sat back and put our feet up. For years, we sent to Brussels the flotsam of Italian politics, along with the odd reasonably well-prepared individual. As our historian will confirm, I'm sure.

Italy is still feeling the effects of those errors. One famous episode, as our economist will know, was the negotiation of the "milk quotas," one of the most vexatious aspects of the common agricultural policy. The Italian delegation arrived with production figures from the 1930s. The delegates from Rome were uncertain whether they should support products from northern Italy, such as milk, butter, and cheese, or those from the south, like wine and olive oil. In the end, they settled for concessions on steel. Overnight, Italy became the world's largest importer of milk. It still is.

Do you want some more recent examples of our contradictory Euroenthusiasm and Eurosloppiness? For years, we held the record for infringements of EC law, and we were unable to exploit European funds Italy was entitled to (we do better these days). In 1995, we agreed to liberalize textile imports from outside Europe. When the new rules went into effect in 2005, we were less prepared for them than any other EU country.

But despite all that, we used to put our faith in Europe, and we still do. The political scientist will tell you that this is a consequence of our distrust for Italian governments, of which we have had fifty-nine, one for each year of the Italian republic's existence. Italians, according to this theory, are so disappointed that any other option looks good.

There's certainly some truth in this. Many of the good things that have been happening recently, such as the reduction of the deficit, a spot of privatization, more competition, and less bureaucracy, came from Brussels, not Rome. The Prodi government shoehorned Italy into the Maastricht parameters by imposing a stiff "Eurotax." Italians paid up without a murmur, simply because it had that name and was for that purpose. In Great Britain, there would have been riots in the streets.

So are we a wise nation that invests in its future? Hold on a minute. Only one Italian in four knew the name of the new currency, and few today have any idea what the proposed European

Constitution is about. Not only that, we find it difficult to be virtuous about our public finances nowadays. And as I have said before, many of us took the opportunity offered by the new currency to jack up prices. Any customer in the hypermarket at this moment would be happy to give you chapter and verse on the subject. Our comedian would appreciate all this.

Do we still love Europe, despite everything? It's hard to give an answer. If you want to know how the story will end, though, a comedian, an economist, a historian, a sociologist, and a marriage consultant are not enough. We'll also need that fortune-teller.

Let's look for one at the frozen-food counter. Anyone who can work out what's in those frozen pancakes must have supernatural powers.

# Day Seven: In Naples

### The sidewalk, or on collective individualism

A Naples sidewalk proves that Italians can ride herd and stay in the saddle. A stroll is a mental rodeo that requires bold professionals. Anything unexpected is a challenge, and no one here wants to admit defeat.

The sidewalk of Corso Umberto is a shopping area, the Spanish Quarter is an attempt at territorial expansion, and the *lungomare*, the beachfront promenade, is a place to observe and meditate. In Via Tasso, the thoroughfare that descends elegantly from Vomero to Riviera di Chiaia, the sidewalk is equally complicated. Pedestrians have to thread their way between fruit crates and window blinds, skipping over large souvenirs left by small dogs, ducking under the washing, and squeezing past interminable lines of parked Vespas. Two are bolted together underneath a sign that says: VEHICLE EN-TRANCE AT ALL TIMES—DAY AND NIGHT—NO PARKING OR WAITING.

133

They're not disturbing anyone. Even if the Vespas were hauled, there would still be two automobiles, which look as if they've been there since Maradona left the local soccer club in 1991.

Naples' anarchy can be interpreted, provided you don't fall into the trap of folklore. Like many great Italian inventions, Naples is exciting. However, it is weighed down by habits that look relaxed but actually generate tension. Avoid romantic absolutions. Many Neapolitans are fed up with them, just as they are fed up with people who refuse to call the Camorra, the local Mafia, by its real name. They are fed up with incomprehensible authority that forces people to beg for what they are entitled to. And they are fed up with a middle class that does things it won't talk about, and says things it doesn't do.

This isn't anarchy. It is the foggy calm that leads to decline. Real Neapolitan anarchy is a manifestation of collective individualism, the kind of paradox that few in the world can pull off. Take this sorry-looking Vespa leaning against the wall. It has not been abandoned. The neglect is a subtle form of camouflage. This way, the scooter won't be noticed, keyed, or stolen.

The seeming confusion of a Naples street is an elaborate form of organization, and shows how the impenetrability of bodies is an opinion, not a law of physics. In some districts, the sidewalk is used to create a dignified entrance for a basement flat by having a porch built on it. On the outskirts of the city, the sidewalk is a dump. Mattresses and boxes wait for the rag-and-bone man, who is a regular visitor. Metal poles placed to stop cars from parking are used for hitching scooters, which are ever-present in a city on a slope that has no use for bicycles. Every pole has its scooter. The owner leaves a chain attached to show who's in charge when the scooter is in use. In areas where traffic is particularly heavy, the sidewalk is a fast lane. Pedestrians know this, and don't use it.

In general, pedestrians in Naples disdain sidewalks. They prefer to walk in the street, so as not to get in the way of other people and their affairs. The sidewalk is the home of the professional beggar, before whom it is forbidden to loiter. Then there are the fake designer bags, neatly laid out on a box that can be used either for transport or instant concealment. You'll find artificial rain, when a gardener just has to water the plants right now. And there are cigarette ends, and marks left by tires or motorcycle stands. Archeologists of the future will study those as soon as they've finished with Pompeii.

Outside schools, bars, and restaurants, the sidewalk is the appointed venue for *intalliamento,* the practice of hanging out while you decide what to do, reflect on life, nibble a snack, and observe the world. This form of hanging out is a fascinating Italian habit. Many foreigners mistake it for indecision, but it's actually a preliminary. It's the anticipation of pleasure, and demands a certain skill.

When a dozen adolescents are chatting outside the Mercalli High School, they are continuing the conversations they were having in class, or IM'ing one another, or tapping out on their laptops. They aren't wasting time. On the sidewalk, they learn, deal, investigate, and establish their pecking orders ("Who's got the voucher for the club?"). The thirty-year-olds outside the Farinella restaurant are studying aesthetics, anthropology, meteorology (it might rain), and crowd psychology all at the same time. They're late because they want to be late. Otherwise, they would have moved off an hour ago. Talking about the journey is as much fun as arriving. If this is neurotic, they don't mind.

When the French writer Roger Peyrefitte passed through (*Du Vésuve à l'Etna,* 1952), he observed, "Italy is the last country where people savor the joy of living. It makes us believe it even when Italy herself has ceased to believe." Half a century later, that observation holds true. Staying in the saddle despite life's buckings is a gratifying exercise. It is no coincidence that Naples generates passion and frustration but not desperation. The struggle has not yet been won, but neither has it been lost.

*   *   *

Italian motorists must—not "like to," not "want to," not "beg to," but absolutely *must*—park right next to their destination, with no thought for the consequences. It's true all over the country, but here in Naples, under pressure from the lack of space, stimulated by the uphill gradients, and excited by the descents, drivers seem to be particularly creative.

Anyone arriving by car expects to park outside the front door. A couple of hundred meters away there may be a huge free parking lot, but that's irrelevant. Leaving the car there would be an admission of defeat. Our car user circles like a shark awaiting the moment to strike. If the individual concerned thinks he or she is important—a title that many in Naples like to acquire in the course of brief, solitary award ceremonies—then irritation increases. Status is inversely proportional to the distance between destination and parking space. The closer the car, the more important the driver.

One hateful variant is the double-parking syndrome. Italy's towns are snarled up by legions of drivers who have, theoretically, "just stopped for a moment." The distinction between "waiting" and "parking," explained in the highway safety code, is the focus of philosophical discussions. How long does "waiting" have to go on before it becomes "parking"? How can you justify parking where you shouldn't and wriggle out of a fine?

It gets worse. Increasingly often in Italian cities, you see unauthorized cars parked in spaces for the disabled, or cars with borrowed or fraudulently obtained permits (watch how the driver skips into the store). In these cases, the remedy lies with the authorities, and should be applied with energy. But the authorities have other things to do. Like parking close to the office.

\* \* \*

Naples has one advantage. There aren't very many SUVs. Cars, scooters, and pedestrians occupy all the available space, and in some of the lanes you simply couldn't get through in an off-road vehicle. Even the in-your-face exhibitionism of some Italians has to admit defeat before the narrowness of the Spanish Quarter streets. The ancient city in the shade of Vesuvius is spared that indignity, at least.

But elsewhere in Italy, SUVs dominate the townscape. On rainy days in Milan, Big American Cars shoot through Small Italian Streets, sending up a spray worthy of a hydrofoil. In the mountains, apparently serious individuals do appalling things. Whipped into a frenzy by four-wheel drives, they crash through banks of snow, park on forty-five-degree inclines, and give displays of countersteering to disgusted local residents.

But it hardly ever snows in Rome or Naples. Motorists need other challenges, such as buying a sub-subcompact, driving it flamboy-antly, and parking it with élan. On the sidewalk, if possible. Look at the people behind the wheel. They know they're driving a down-sized vehicle, so they loosen up and slither into the narrowest of gaps. Often they are middle-aged men with an odd light in their eyes. It's not a Smart they're driving: it's a Batmobile. They rush at the steep streets of the Vomero as if they were the avenues of Gotham City.

There's another category of motorists that deserve examination here in Naples. I'm talking about the Potential Driver, who has found a parking space—improbable, improvised, or just plain impermissible—and has no intention of giving it up. This driver gets around on foot, on a scooter, or on public transport, defying ticket inspectors and muggers. But the car stays where it is. Every so often, he dusts the vehicle off. Why should he move it? A car is a form of reassurance, proof of prosperity, and a place to listen to the radio or store wine. No one around here has ever parked so close to home before. The neighbors know this, and observe in admiration.

## The automobile, and fumbling on the fold-down seats

Look at the skeptical smile on that guy's face. He is incapable of imagining anything in the world except the perpendicular line that joins his car to the sky. No, that's not one of mine. The image comes from the Catalan writer Montalbán, but it's just as good in Naples as it is in Barcelona. Take a glance at that Italian face admiring itself in the rearview mirror, in love with the instruments on the dashboard, safe in the air-conditioned interior. It's the face of an extreme parking expert, always ready to unleash a threatening scowl or a magnanimous smile.

Traffic is fun, pointed out Neapolitan writer Luciano De Crescenzo in *Thus Spake Bellavista*. But that was thirty years ago, and I get the impression that Neapolitans aren't having quite so good a time these days. Naturally, in some parts of town they continue to toot their horns to feel they're not alone (another observation from *Bellavista*), but they'd prefer not to have to spend their afternoons backed up at intersections, waiting for the person at the front of the line to decide whether it's preferable to go with the green light and risk hitting someone who has jumped a red, or to jump the red in the knowledge that the other cars have a green.

This sort of abstruse lucubration is exclusively Italian. People think like that in Milan, too, but in Naples the reasoning has an esoteric dimension. Though I don't believe it, there's an urban legend that says when the pedestrian lines fade away they aren't repainted: they might encourage someone's suicidal presumption that you can step off the sidewalk without looking. Where there aren't any lines, things are left up to the sharpness of the pedestrian's eye and the generosity of the motorist's heart. Both are in plentiful supply in Naples.

• • •

In Italy, there are seventy-two cars for every one hundred residents. Most of the larger European countries average two people for each vehicle. We're on a par with the U.S.A., but we don't have the U.S.A.'s open spaces, which is why Italians are generally better at parking than Americans. Parking spaces are scarce, gas prices and insurance premiums are rising, and the roads simply can't cope. The ever-jammed beltway around Mestre, on the mainland opposite Venice, is a subtle form of humor. The Autosole between Florence and Bologna is a horror movie, and the *autostrada* that snakes from Salerno to Reggio Calabria has been called a "cart track" by its own management company. And what do we do? We buy a new car. In January 2005, 212,568 vehicles were registered, along with 45,569 births. It shows where our priorities lie.

Naples is no different. People drive no more than a few thousand kilometers a year. Cars aren't used for transport. They just mean you can be as comfortable as you are at home, doing the things you do at home. Otherwise, there's the scooter. Some of the more acrobatic families manage to circulate four at a time on the same bike. Helmet-less, of course, so that they can salute the crowd. Cars are one way to talk to your children on the school run, even if it's only a quarter-mile, or to take your bathing hut to the seaside with you, or to see without being seen, or to be seen without being examined. In Naples, cars rarely go to the junkyard. They appear, disappear, are taken apart, and are put together again like a conjurer's trick.

Cars are no longer an Italian's calling card, as they were in the past. If anything, they are an extension of the womb that comes af-ter the stroller and before the easy chair. They're not even a means of transport. They're a means to something else. The problem is finding out what. Status? No model can guarantee that, but some cars bespeak purchasing power, and for many people that's enough.

Italian marques have ceased to identify social groups, as they once did. Fiat compacts were for the working class, Lancia sedans for the middle classes and the quiet life, and Alfa Romeos for young-sters, or fifty-year-olds who aspired to look young. In today's Italy, youth is a constitutional right, the middle classes are restless, the working class has disappeared, and Fiat has had a tough time, too.

The automobile has become a private place, where quirks and fantasies intertwine. Bodywork maniacs are becoming extinct, espe-cially in Naples, where keeping the paintwork intact is like playing defensive end with a lit candle in one hand. You can try, but it ain't easy. On the other hand, the alternative uses of the car are growing. In our automobiles, we telephone, argue, deal, wait, drink, confess our sins, warm our hands, slake our thirsts, listen to music, catch up on the news, and fiddle with the instruments. Men study the effect they make in sunglasses. Women put on makeup, and woe betide anyone who tries to hurry them up. A few smoke, because they can't in the office or the bar, but more and more ashtrays are full of small change for the *autostrada* tolls, and they don't smell so bad.

Finally, Italian cars are still where people woo and seduce. For some people, performance *in* a car is more important than the performance *of* a car. If you're young and have limited space at home, your car is a sort of bedroom on wheels. It has always been like that, since the days of the tiny Fiat Cinquecento, which delivered comfort-free romance and a hand brake in the lower back. This sort of thing goes on more in the south of Italy than in the north, for reasons of climate, accommodations, and family circumstance. In fact, fold-down fumbling is one of the great traditions of Naples. It has its own cadences, rules, and venues. The bold repair to the wilder suburbs, and romantics opt for the beachfront. Many would use the parking lots, but the public ones are too busy, and private parking costs money. Any couple that has a garage can afford a hotel, which is much more comfortable.

* * *

To be popular in Italy, a car has to look good on the driver. In fact, it has to become sensuous, by virtue of its shape and its advertising. Engine, fuel consumption, equipment, and instrumentation are all secondary to the excitement of the first impression. Cars should confirm the flattering image we have of ourselves. As you will have realized, this is no easy enterprise.

Volvo has found new fans thanks to the XC90, a sturdy-looking SUV. For some Italians, the Scandinavian understatement of the classic station wagon was vaguely disappointing. The aerodynamic, futuristic, aluminum-built Audi A2 did not sell well here. No metal is sexy in Italy, apart from titanium, which has a nice name. A while back, Volkswagen tried to export an advertising campaign to Italy. The star was a sedan speeding through the rain. The campaign worked in Germany, but here it was taken off almost at once. Italians don't buy cars because the windshield wipers are efficient. Rain depresses us.

142 Beppe Severgnini

After a period in the doldrums, Alfa Romeo made a comeback with the 156, which men love. It's a feminine car with curvy lines, like the actress that emerged from the trunk clutching her shoes in the commercial. Then came the 147, which is popular with women. It's masculine, with an assertive look. Finally, there was the GT, a shameless reference to the Giulietta, a sexy, staid Lombard car with a Shakespearean name.

Fiat boosted profits with the Punto, and continues to sell the excellent Panda after nearly eliminating it from the range. When the new version came out, the management in Turin wanted to call it the "Gingo." It was a crazy idea and a silly name, as if the British were to rechristen the Mini "Polly."

The Lancia Ypsilon is another deeply Italian automobile. "Sky Dome Sunroof/Glamour Trim/DFN Dolce Far Niente Gearshift" says the advertising. "You see her. You get in. You go out with her. Innovative, elegant, sporting the traditional Lancia style notes with sensual modern appeal," the copy promises. "Titian Red, Vivaldi Blue, De Chirico Azure, Botticelli Gray," recites the color palette. There's a whole existential design in the nonchalant sprinkling of English words. There's an illusion of seduction in the identification with the female, and extravagance in the combinations of history and color. But the car sells, which perhaps isn't surprising.

Summing up, then, we could say that buying a car in Italy is a form of self-expression and a token of belonging. Do you know why there are so many cars, especially big sedans, with metallic paint? It's because silver is the color of the Wealthy Club. It's a subliminal clique, which no one will consciously admit to having joined. A sort of reassuring Rotary of the mind, it attracts businessmen, pharmacists, sales reps, and young professionals. Once, blue cars were popular for the same reason. If you were lucky, people might mistake your car for a government minister's.

•  •  •

Popular classics are rare, but nations know how to recognize them. Take the Fiat Seicento. Fifty years ago, it was launched as the *utilitaria*, or subcompact. The Italian name was a declaration of intent: useful rather than good-looking. It cost 590,000 lire, the equivalent of ten months' salary for a factory worker, five for an office worker, two for a journalist, or one for a business executive. For a down payment of fifty thousand lire, it was yours. The rest could be paid off in installments. When the Seicento came out in 1955, there was one car for every seventy-seven Italians (in France, the ratio was one to fourteen). By 1957, there was a car for every thirty-nine people. After acquiring their refrigerator, or rather *Frigidaire,* Italians decided to spend their savings on a Seicento.

When the Fiat Cinquecento came out a couple of years later, it, too, was exciting, and not just because the forward-opening doors enabled bystanders to admire the legs of emerging females. The Cinquecento has an image we identify with, just as Germans do with the Beetle. But the Cinquecento became the people's car without having to call itself a "Volkswagen." It's a souvenir of the way we were at an epic moment in our history. In 1957, Italy discovered the European Community, the Champions' Cup, and the televisual ritual of *Carosello,* the advertising broadcast. The Cinquecento was the fourth "C" of a new age. It may not have been a Renaissance, or even a Risorgimento. Perhaps it was just a Renewal, but it was needed.

To look original, a bright color, or a sunroof and a couple of customized seat-covers, was all it took. Italians weren't really looking for a car that would make them unique. What they wanted, and what they still want, is reassurance, encouragement, and a touch of style. If, fifty years ago, Turin had turned out the equivalent of the

Prinz 600—an extralarge Spam can—then the history of Italy could well have been different. Fiat's certainly would have been.

* * *

After the Second World War, we Italians wore blue jeans and felt almost American. You Americans hopped onto a scooter and felt a teensy bit Italian. One after another, Hollywood stars had their photos taken on a Vespa, among them William Holden, James Stewart, Charlton Heston, Anthony Quinn, Gary Cooper. A scooter was Gregory Peck's preferred means of adding excitement to Audrey Hepburn's Roman holiday. No helmets in those days. The wind in your hair was more important than personal safety.

In the same period, a Hungarian transplanted to London called George Mikes was writing *How to Be an Alien,* a book in which he made gentle fun of his new compatriots. Mikes came to Italy and wrote *Italy for Beginners,* in which the still relatively new Vespa had a place of honor. According to Mikes, its meaning was (a) sexual, (b) social, and (c) political. The first point is particularly interesting.

Mikes writes:

> You see the lovely, dark Italian girls riding their Vespas, showing lots of leg. Their function is to distract the attention of motorists from the road. Not that the Italian driver paid too much attention to the road in the past; today however he pays still less. These modern Vespal Virgins keep an eternal light aglow; and many sacrifices of various kinds (human life included), are made on their altars.

"The social significance of the Vespa is about as great in postwar Italy as the Model T Ford was in the United States in the twenties. It brings motoring to the masses," adds Mikes. That's true. Unlike the Cinquecento, which took its time getting established, the Vespa was an instant hit, because it enabled people to change their routine. Italians could get to work quicker, and take their girlfriends into the countryside at the weekend. All you needed was a plaid travel rug—another Italian icon of the period, and an object that deserves further study.

The first Vespa was made in 1946. The Piaggio factory at Pontedera in Tuscany had been making aircraft, but after the war it had to invent a new product or risk closure. Then someone remembered the little scooters used by parachutists in the airports, and had an idea. Why not use the starter motors left over in the warehouses to make a low-cost vehicle with an unusual-looking body (reminiscent of a wasp, or *vespa* in Italian)? It worked better than anyone expected. The architect Vittorio Gregotti wrote: "Italian design was capable of bridging, with a brilliant aesthetic solution, the gaps in a manufacturing base that still presented huge imbalances of consumption, and was technologically and organizationally mature, but often haphazard in its methodology." As if to say imagination is useful and recklessness helps. Even then, Italians knew how to make a virtue out of necessity.

The Vespa had the advantages of a motorbike, including low fuel consumption, low bulk, and the thrill of the wind in your hair, but none of the inconveniences, since it was light and relatively quiet, you could ride it in a skirt, and it kept the mud off. In the 1950s, Vespas were available in Lancia showrooms, alongside the stylish Appia. The millionth Piaggio scooter was sold in 1956, and it cost a third of a Seicento. The star of ninety films, hijacked by Prime Minister Alcide De Gasperi ("My government deserves the credit for giving the motor scooter to the people"), and praised by Pius XII

("The scooter has raised the living standards of social classes that cannot afford more expensive vehicles"), the Vespa proves that when we Italians keep it simple we are unbeatable.

It's our love of Baroque that gets us into trouble.

## The travel agency, where the nation flexes its flippancy and pampers its patriotism

A journey begins before the departure. A journey is in the mind of the would-be traveler, and, as you'll have worked out, the Italian mind is an exotic location that deserves a guided tour. You can bank on the fact that anyone who goes into a travel agency wants something special. There's no such thing as a package tour in Italy. Even the smallest group—the couple—is the sum of two distinct journeys, each with its own ends. Not all of which can be openly admitted, of course.

A family organizing a weekend in a foreign city never has just one schedule. There'll be someone wanting to see the museums, and someone interested in the restaurants, the panoramas, or the romance. Some will want to leave again as soon as they get there. What's more, the characteristics of Italian travelers turn up in bizarre combinations. Pick 'n' mix from conformism, curiosity, wisdom, rashness, offhandedness as a way of life, shrewd generosity, timid exhibitionism, prodigal parsimony, and demure patriotism. In Naples, they add a bit of excess and lots of imagination: people from the south are exponentially Italian. But those are the ingredients.

Let's watch this lady leafing through a catalogue. She's tempted by the palm trees, which at any latitude in Italy are the hallmark of the new Orientalism, even when they actually lie to the west. The points of the compass have never been our strong point. The lady is unable to locate the isles of her dreams on a map, but she is reassured by the palms leaning over the white sands, totally forgetting that there are plenty of such trees along Via Caracciolo in Naples. Now she's discovered that her friends are going to the same resort. Her joy is complete. Enjoyment is ensured.

Lots of towns in Italy move around in this way, heading for this year's hot spot of the century. Naples loves Cuba and Santo Domingo in the winter. In the summer, Neapolitans meet up on Corfu or Formentera, having bumped into each other on Ischia, and in the expectation of seeing everyone again on Capri. Half of Rome rendezvouses on Ibiza in the summer. Wealthy Milanese meet up for an apéritif in the Maldives in wintertime.

What is the saving grace of those who take part in these mass migrations? Their curiosity, as we said. Well, they want to be involved, to conspire, comment, find out, compare, and purchase something, a partner, a restaurant, or a museum. Their inevitable comments contain flashes of genius and pieces of perversion. The only place in the world we keep our mouths shut is the desert. Unless, of course, we have a camcorder, and want to add a sound track. In which case, we don't shut up even there.

● ● ●

Let's move on to wisdom and rashness. We'll start by saying that traveling has always reflected the spirit of the age, from the Grand Tour to the All-Inclusive Tour. I remember the 1980s and those last Italian holidaymakers who went around in groups led by a dictatorial guide. They would cross Manhattan for a plate of pasta. Today it's different. Italian tourists have turned into travelers, albeit imperfect ones. They don't take things lying down. They act and react.

Listen to the guy over there who wants to take his dog to China. Nothing's going to stop him, not even the possibility that his pet might end up as an appetizer.

The bravado vanishes when things begin to cost. Italians have a left-field form of parsimony that takes strange forms. Some people use travel agents to make four or five bookings, but don't buy a ticket. Others take heaps of brochures, treating them as complimentary magazines. Still others come to discuss destinations they have no intention of visiting, but the destination allows them to show off a little erudition, which is always nice. Just listen to him. His kids are waiting for him in Lombardy while he's complaining, "It costs less to get to New York than to Milan!" Anywhere else, he'd restrict himself to making the observation, but a Neapolitan might just catch a transatlantic flight out of spite, or a sudden desire for a holiday.

"Innocents Abroad" was what Mark Twain called American travelers, having spied on their excursions. "Improvidents Abroad" might be a good title for a modern Italian version. Audiovisual aids are a must. No writer would be able to describe the face of a guy from Milan visiting San Francisco in summertime only to discover it's as foggy as Lodi in the fall. Comments on Prague are equally interesting. It's a city that Italians go wild over, even if no one can explain why. What comes out is a mixed salad of romance and literature in which Kafka is the tomato but no one knows the names of the greens.

Now we come to the travelers' flippancy, which is persevering, professional, and perky. That couple over there have decided how they're going to spend the money from their wedding-list, which lots of newlyweds here in Naples leave at the travel agency, earning a sorry-looking basket of fruit in their room on arrival. They've opted for Egypt, but they won't be reading up on the country before they depart. They'll take with them recollections from their school-days, popular films, and television documentaries, hoping to get by on their instincts. What's the problem? Well, their instincts really do work. The newlyweds from Naples will work out how to deal with boatmen on the Nile two days before a couple from Cleveland, and twenty-four hours ahead of a pair from Paris. This will merely convince them that it is pointless to prepare for a trip. Then, of course, they'll confuse Abu Simbel and Abu Dhabi. As the Americans and the French, who have pored over the guidebook, will be sure to point out.

What about the shrewd generosity? There are lots of examples, such as those generous tips to get special treatment, the thoughtfulness to children they don't know, who are then punished by having to pose for photos, and the attempts to be useful even when they are only getting in the way. Every Italian abroad feels like a conjurer, a missionary, a diplomat, a statesperson, an anthropologist, and a secret agent. And, up to a point, they actually are. They may offer simple solutions to complex problems, but they do so with such enthusiasm that you can't take offense. A group of Italians in Cairo, the Caribbean, Bangkok, or Brazil is a sort of glorified school trip. The tour guide has the thankless task of being the teacher at the front of the bus.

Finally, there's that prodigal parsimony. Whatever the case, Italians don't cut corners on travel. They might decide not to buy a suit, or descend on discount stores to stock up on products with improbable names. But they have no intention of staying in the same place. The young and the enterprising have discovered budget airlines. They're the ones yawning after an all-nighter at the airport, wearing windcheaters and woolly hats, and clutching a bottle of mineral water. The rest of the middle class, pushed ever nearer the poverty line by superfluous gadgetry and commercials, goes into a travel agency looking for bargains. Who said only the aristocracy knew how to decline in style?

＊　＊　＊

They were still there at three in the morning, with dawn creeping up on the palms of Bahia. A tableful of forty-year-old Italians with dazzling smiles, loud voices, standard-issue polo shirts, and deck shoes was entertaining a swarm of young Brazilian girls. One Italian was commenting on a female backside swaying to the rhythm of the *pagode*. Its owner was laughing. Why not? He was paying, after all. He wasn't paying much, actually, only 150 realls (50 euros) for the night. Plus drinks, of course.

They were in a bar at Itapúa, on the Atlantic coast north of Salvador, but it could have been a club at Copacabana or Phuket, some of the nightspots in Moscow, many of the restaurants in Cuba, or any number of hotels in Romania. The color of the girls' skin changes, as do the prices and the drinks: *caipiroska* in Moscow, *caipirinha* in Bahia. But the Italians are always the same: numerous and welcome. They don't drink, don't sweat, and don't raise their hands in anger. They're self-controlled, clean, and polite. They laugh, give little gifts, remember names, and say hello the morning after.

In short, we're famous. We trot the poverty-sticken and post-dictatorial globe. There's not much to it. If she's in a shack and he's in a hotel, that's all it takes. At a certain point in the evening, she'll ask in Italian if she can sleep in a bed with clean sheets, instead of sharing a room with her brothers and sisters. And he'll say yes, imagining her stepping out of the shower and happy to have found a cover story for his conscience (but not his wife, of course).

You ought to see those Improvidents Abroad, radiantly happy behind the ice and lemon of their dry *caipirinhas*. They're kinder than the Germans, more numerous than the Americans, and more generous than the Scandinavians. Is this sexual tourism? It certainly is. But you don't need to go to the other side of the world to spend a couple of hours with a girl. You go to feel rich, good-looking, generous, and admired. In other words, you leave Italy to feel more Italian.

●  ●  ●

Another thing you have to learn is that when Italians meet up abroad we like one another. We recognize other Italians in seaports, airports, stations, and trains, in the street markets of London, and on the streetcars of San Francisco, where we're the ones who want to ride hanging on to the car and get told off. On crowded tour buses, Venetians and Sicilians sit side by side. They swap regional recipes instead of arguing about north and south. Back at the hotel in the evening, they tell one another about their shopping expeditions, and show off their trophies. The squabbles of home are forgotten. Everyone seems happy to be Italian, to speak the same language, and to be complaining about the same things.

Compare this with foreigners who meet up in Italy. A couple from Cleveland go into a small restaurant on Capri. They find another two American couples. How do they know they're American? They aren't talking, and don't understand the staff. The two couples see the new couple. Eight eyes glance. Four glance back. Six individuals are studying, classifying, and disliking one another. Yet they're all Americans, and used to social living. Why are they so irritated? After all, the restaurant is indicated in some guide with a name like *Undiscovered Eateries in Italy's South* on sale at bookstores all over the United States. They may be thinking, "Back home, we're good neighbors. Allow us to push our good-neighborliness to the back of the drawer while we're here."

Italians are the exact opposite. Our homes, as you have seen, are guarded by more razor wire than Guantánamo. People are needlessly distrustful, and take issue with everything from the government to politics, ethics, judges, TV, and the AC Milan soccer club. Often all at the same time, thanks to the prime minister. But once we cross the border, all that is forgotten. Why? It might be the novelty of the situation. Abroad, you take a break from your admirable civic sense, and we use the trip to take time out from our enervating cynicism.

# Day Eight: In Sardinia

## The waterfront, the convoluted charm of a liquid frontier

There are towns that should be seen in the morning from the sea. Come up on deck and learn to read the Sardinian port of Cagliari. Look at the towers of the powerful, keeping a watchful eye on each other. There's the city hall, there's the university, and the dome belongs to the cathedral. On the right is the Church of Nostra Signora di Bonaria. Next to it, and built in the same stone, is the home of Renato Soru, the Internet magnate who moved on to regional politics. New and old come together. It's a question of habit, tradition, and reassurance.

Today Cagliari looks different from when the Saracens came to plunder it, when the British came to bombard it, when the Spanish wanted to exploit it, and when the Piedmontese decided to neglect it. But they all sailed up to this harbor, just like us this morning. Their boats were caravels or brigantines; ours is a ferry from the mainland, the *continente*. That's what they call the rest of Italy in Sardinia: "peninsula" would sound too familiar.

Cagliari's harbor is a thousand years old. It's never been very important, perhaps because Sardinians distrust the coast. You can sympathize, considering that the sea has generally brought them trouble, in the shape of pirates, malaria, and colonizers. Over the centuries, though, some well-intentioned seafarers have also arrived. In the fifteenth century, there were traders from Catalonia, Majorca, and Valencia. Then, when Spain began to turn its eyes to the New World, more entrepreneurs landed, from Naples, Sicily, Corsica, Tuscany, and France.

At that time, the Marina district—that's it in front of us, with the yellow, gray, and cyclamen housefronts—was the most modern and best served in the whole town. Workshops and inns opened for business, but the good times didn't last. Spanish taxes and buccaneers from the Low Countries, Britain, and the Barbary Coast quenched entrepreneurial enthusiasm. In 1720, Sardinia passed to the house of Savoy, and was annexed to the kingdom of Piedmont. But the Piedmontese didn't have much interest in the harbor, either. They were happy if it shipped the salt they needed to the mainland.

Little has changed. There's a bit of trade, and a lot of smoke and mirrors over the Porto Canale project. First proposed forty years ago, in ten years' time it will—or, rather, might—enable large container ships to transfer their cargoes to smaller vessels. This shows that Cagliari is in no hurry. It's another case of middle-class lethargy, different from the aristocratic detachment of Palermo but no less fascinating. Both cities know how to wait, and no one can convince them that waiting is not always a good idea.

Cagliari Harbor is a sort of challenge to the sea. Until just a few years ago, a wall separated the quayside from the street. They've knocked the wall down, but this area looks like an unfinished work. It's an Italian weakness, particularly in the south. Very little cargo passes through, yet we're in the center of the Mediterranean. There's only one daily ferry, which goes to Civitavecchia, on the coast north of Rome. Other connections leave once a week for Naples, Livorno, Palermo, Trapani, and Tunis. Peter Gregory-Jones, an English teacher who has been living here for twenty-five years, wrote that he saw the locals crowding the harbor, complete with band, on only one occasion. That was when the Cagliari soccer team was playing away at Naples, and there were plenty of ferries.

Look over there, at the end of Via Baylle. The street with the porticoes is Via Roma. Until the 1940s, it was where the locals took their evening stroll. On the left is the Rinascente department store. Today the area is largely patronized by students, pensioners, and out-of-towners, who enjoy spending an hour sitting at the plastic tables. Note the atmosphere of barely perceptible decline. Scrutinize the shop signs: optician, cell-phone top-ups, pharmacy, lottery office, restaurant, café, and tobacconist. It's a rhythm you'll have to remember if you want to go beyond the tunes of Tuscany.

Poetto, the beach that towel-toting city kids used to take the streetcar to, is Cagliari's only metaphorical truce with the sea. It's a strange, beautiful place. There are no hotels or boarding houses, only Art Deco bathing centers and the usual land's-end atmosphere of southern Sardinia. And the fragrance of eucalyptus among the kiosks, bar tables, and dark sand. The sand was the local council's idea, but Cagliari residents don't like it. They preferred it when it was white, and a better match for the green of the water and the blue of the sky.

⚫ ⚫ ⚫

As in many other seaports, at Cagliari new arrivals occupy the no-man's-land near the harbor. Here, as elsewhere, there is the usual cocktail of dejection, drive, getting by, and going under as Albania meets Morocco, Senegal, and China.

On the right, opposite the fishing boats and between the railway and bus stations, is Piazza Matteotti with its bust of Giuseppe Verdi. A socialist and a composer watch over the imported poor and the odd local hothead. On the left, near the ENEL building that awkwardly shuts off the view of the promenade, is Piazza Darsena, a meeting place for Ukrainian women employed to care for the old. Every Saturday, a small bus leaves for Kiev, taking parcels to their families across the sea, the Italian peninsula, Austria, and Slovakia. A full-time carer earns six hundred euros a month. An Italian would cost five times as much, including taxes and Social Security contributions.

It's like that all over Italy. In the bars first thing in the morning, you see couples made up of an old person and a companion—the former Italian, the latter from abroad. In the afternoon, Italy's parks are populated by babysitters with children, and domestic servants walking dogs. We sit in the restaurants in the evening, but they're working in the kitchen. In the suburbs, only the new arrivals walk. Italians cruise past in cars, surprised to find pedestrians where there didn't use to be any.

Two and a half million immigrants with residence permits live in Italy, plus an unknown number of illegal ones. Here in Cagliari, you see them scurrying along Via Roma with their eyes lowered, clutching an ugly bag. There are Africans who have crossed the sea, South Americans who have crossed the world, and Asians who have abandoned their overcrowded cities. They should have entered Italy legally, but it didn't turn out that way. The influx has been chaotic, often tragic, and there have been five immigration amnesties in less than twenty years. Still, these people are here now. And we don't really know what to do.

Some Italians seek immigrants to pay them less, to treat them badly, to be able to fire them when they feel like it, and to hire them again if they see fit. Agriculture in the south survives on this seasonal, flexible, obedient labor force, but in Valle d'Aosta, at the other end of Italy, a couple was charged with enslaving a Moroccan, forcing him to look after livestock for eighteen hours a day. All over the country, apparently respectable people boast about hiring disposable domestics paid strictly in cash, with no contract. Fortunately, most Italians pay honest wages and offer decent living conditions. They are the Italians who remember that, until not so very long ago, we were the needy migrants.

But lazy lawmaking threatens to cause problems. Immigration has to be regulated and explained. Otherwise, the ignorant and the ill-intentioned will find a pretext. Immigration here is not a hangover from colonialism, as it is in Great Britain, France, or Holland. In Italy, immigration is an economic necessity, and an accident of geography. Our peninsula hangs like a ripe fruit over the heads of the poor in Africa, the Balkans, and the Near East. There are jobs that we don't want to do anymore but immigrants will.

Immigration is a sensitive issue. It deserves a plan, perhaps not as revolutionary as the American one, as methodical as Canada's, as radical as Australia's, or as rational as Japan's. It just has to be clear and assimilation-friendly. Instead, we give the new arrivals a job, but deny them respect or rights. Or we grant them rights, but fail to remind them of their obligations. For example, millions of people around the world who have Italian ancestors have been promised an Italian passport. To earn it, they don't even have to learn Italian, which is still the nation's most powerful glue.

In contrast, newcomers to the United States find a radical option: the country is peopled by immigrants, the melting pot is still bubbling away, and the future is something that most people want to build together. It would be naïve to attempt to do that in Italy. Our minestrone has been simmering for a thousand years, and has a flavor of its own. But we can add new ingredients, not least because Italy is growing old and needs new energy.

Some of that energy is sitting here at the plastic tables in Via Roma, taking in the situation.

## The beach, a bare outline

Unlike the Swiss or the Swedes, we Italians do not have an idyllic image of our country. Nor do we have a self-image as epic as the American, Russian, or Polish ones. Our picture of Italy is a party. What we aspire to is gratifying chaos.

That's why we're here today. The beach is a good outline sketch of Italy. Get changed, look around, and don't worry if people stare at you. On a summer afternoon, there are all sorts here. You'll see preening, momentary solidarity, unintentional elegance, body care, love of detail, boundary-watching, the subtle tyranny of children, and secrets shared with strangers.

Each shadow is a group, and each group has its own hierarchy. Some talk, others listen. Some declaim, others interrupt. Some observe, and others let them. Your neighbors shouldn't be too close or you'd feel hemmed in. Nor should they be too far away or you'd feel isolated. There is a preferred Italian distance, which is less than the British one and greater than the Japanese version.

A beach in Italy is not just a prelude to the sea, which in many places—though luckily not in Sardinia—is almost an irrelevance. The beach is a catwalk, a gallery, a gym, a track, a restaurant, a market, a workshop, a sauna, a reading room, a place of meditation, and sufficiently off-limits to be an exciting place to take your date. It's a crowded space where some people go to be on their own. It's a theater of familial self-sufficiency.

Look at those three generations—grandparents, daughter, and grandchildren—installed under two beach umbrellas with their picnic in cooler bags. They're looking at the sea and the other people, working out when to take a swim, and seeking a balance between enjoying life and striving to improve it.

•  •  •

We are at Is Arutas, on the Sinis Peninsula. This is Italy's Far West, if ever there was one. Down there, the Phoenician ruins of Tharros slither into the sea. Look at that marvelous white beach, the black rocks, the blue sky, and the green water. Quartz and basalt are present in just the right proportions, the sun is in front of us, and there's water all around. This is a free beach. Remember that when you go back to the peninsula and have to pay, or haggle, to get into one of the five thousand bathing centers, despite the fact that the sea belongs to everyone and is accessible to all by law.

Try swimming parallel to the beach. Imagine it's the opening scene of a film, with a Robert Altman–style shot over the water. Observe the Italians. The young people you can see are Sardinians from Cabras, Oristano, and Iglesias. Some, like us today, have come from Cagliari. They're sitting in groups or pairs, standing in the shallows, or strolling along the water's edge. They're bright, polite, fun to be with, and apparently happy. They talk; they don't shout. They discuss but don't squabble. The boys watch the girls, and the girls watch back. There are no scowls, no smells, no noises, no fried foods, no sweat stains, no rubbish, and no hangovers. There are microscopic bikinis and brightly colored thongs, but no naked breasts. The girls flaunt what they've got, but with modesty.

Yet this is a public beach. This is supposed to be the infernal south of Italy, which fascinated and terrified the travelers of Northern Europe. Something isn't quite right.

Some of the credit goes to the beach itself, a forum for socialization that is almost as congenial to Italians as it is to Brazilians. But some also goes to the people who come here. They may not be perfect, but, like many young Italians, they speak better, drink less, smile more, and have more self-assurance than their contemporaries in other countries. What's more, they love Italy. It's not an aggressive love, or a grouchy one. Let's just say they're content with what they see, eat, touch, and dream of. They're a little less happy about the things they see going wrong, and the promises people make to them. But they've decided to stay, and live their lives on the frontier.

    • • •

The names are similar, and they're very close to each other, but Is Arenas is different from Is Arutas. There's smooth quartz at Is Arenas, and dunes of fine sand here. Is Arenas had parking lots. Is Arutas offers three campsites and unpretentious pizzerias on the edge of the pine wood that was planted to halt the progress of the sand. A swath of smells sneaks past the automobiles, many from abroad and all overloaded. Pine resin mingles with juniper, figs, brine, eucalyptus, steam, fried foods, and sunblock. The sand is white and the sunlight apricot. If this were our only contribution to Europe, it wouldn't be a bad one.

I've brought you to Sardinia because I know it and I like it. It's a large island, crossed by the fortieth parallel, and accounts for one-twelfth of Italy's surface area. There are 1,650,000 people living here. They are not the live-in custodians of a theme park with swimming pools, as some of those who have only seen the Costa Smeralda on the Web may think. They're Italians with problems, passions, interests, desires, fixations, and the odd sloppy trait. The *nuraghi,* prehistoric towers built with large blocks of stone, are a perfect metaphor for the Sardinian psychology, which is sturdy, reliable, defensive, and mysterious.

For reasons of numbers, history, and local culture—which is pastoral, not seagoing—Sardinians have not despoiled their coastline, as has happened in Calabria and Sicily. We mainland Italians have done most, and the worst, of the damage. In the past thirty years, the coastline has sprouted holiday villages, signs of neglect, and labels. Why must any decent beach be christened "Tahiti," as if Sardinia were just another Polynesia?

This south of Italy is not a theme park. Yet neither is it a quiet, boring corner for cultured foreigners, snobbish Italians, old people, or families with children. It's a lively, pungently perfumed place. It's the road to Oristano, an odd-shaped rock, a juniper bush, a strawberry tree, a local paper, and a restaurant that stays open all year round. It's mountains and picnics on the beach. It's a land that craves water. It's work for the people holidaymakers never see, and who never take holidays of their own. It's an insistent, essential wind.

This is Italy's frontier. Admire it, you who come here from afar, and pray for it not to be devastated. Hope that it invents an economy for itself, because the solutions adopted so far—including mines, heavy industry, and second homes—have left mainly scars. Convince southern Italy that it can become Europe's wellness center, provided it sets up services, obeys rules, and fights off local bullies and imported rogues. Promise that you won't adore the island for the three months of summer and forget about it for the rest of the year.

Regions and partners don't like it when you treat them like that.

* * *

One summer sport that costs nothing and guarantees entertainment is observing foreign families with children and comparing them with Italian families. The aim is to investigate child-rearing, not to award scores.

Has the German kid just eaten? He goes into the water, even if the sea is rough and there are more red flags flying than at a party rally in Beijing. The Italian child will be under the beach umbrella, listening to his stomach to work out whether he has digested his lunch. Is the sun blazing down? The little Dutch girl, red as a beet, is making sand castles at the waterline, while her Italian contemporary has on so much sunblock that if her mother tried to hug her she'd pop out like a bar of soap. Is the weather inclement? The British kid skips off singing in the rain, and the Italian stays home. Or emerges kitted out like a deep-sea diver, even though he's in the mountains.

The same is true of traveling. Northern European families move to Spartan rhythms and systems. They may be in a BMW X5, but you get the impression that the kids would get out to push if the car broke down. Take a look at the Italian families. Their style is more Athenian. Everything is examined, discussed, and negotiated.

Perhaps too much. Many Italian parents show a curious resignation, and a mind-boggling faith in divine Providence. You see newborns in their mothers' arms in the front passenger seats, three-year-olds struggling with seatbelts round their necks, and carseats purchased by one family in two, fitted by one in three, and used by one in five. And rear seatbelts? Elsewhere in the Western world, children are forced to wear them. In Italy, they are looked on as a sort of straitjacket, and we leave our kids unbelted. Our children risk injuring their heads because, metaphorically at least, we their parents have completely lost ours.

* * *

The Ferragosto holiday on August 15 is a long way off, but you ought to know what it is and what it's like. It's a festival that puzzles non-Italians. You don't understand what we're celebrating. The end of summer? No, it's too early. The peak of the high season? No, it's too late. We make too much noise for anyone to concentrate on the Assumption of Our Lady, and we're too anxious to make August 15 into a full-blown party. Then there's the vaguely metallic name, Ferragosto. The *agosto* (August) bit is fair enough, but what is *ferro* (iron) doing there? Once, I heard a theory that involved red-hot metal. It's not right, but it's just as intriguing as *feria d'agosto* (August holiday).

At the beginning of every summer, we read learned articles in the papers about staggering vacation periods, "hit-and-run" holidays, and "reasonable" departure times (it's stretching a point to call them "intelligent"). Then Ferragosto comes round, and everything is the same as last year. People flee their homes, if they possibly can. We hit all right, but only if they won't let us run down an overcrowded *autostrada*. It's not clear whether we are forced to go because offices and shops are closed, or whether we don't want to forsake a collective ritual with the barbarian overtones of crowds, lines, waits, torments, and complaints.

I'm beginning to suspect that the mass exodus is Italy's Ferragosto. The rest is just vacations. You're not supposed to relax at Ferragosto; you take part. After all, every nation has evolved its own kind of relaxation. Germany's relaxation is packed with trips, drinking, and regrets. America's doesn't exist. In the States, they even invented rocking chairs, so you can keep moving while you're sitting still. France's relaxation is languid. Britain's is deceptive. There are always minds at work in the English and Scottish countryside, even if there is no P. G. Wodehouse or Evelyn Waugh to describe them. But Italian relaxation is communal and obsessive. Few in this country know how to relax without emerging the worse for wear.

Places to "relax"—a word that has a threatening, switchblade sound when pronounced Italian-style—have been taken over by the legions of the eternally active. First it was the seaside, occupied by athletes and nightflies. Then it was the turn of the mountains and the spas, invaded by health fanatics. Finally, it was the turn of the religious sanctuaries and monasteries, where you often find hectic trading or hastily organized conferences. Even the countryside and the hill country, where it seemed possible to do nothing, are swarming with amateur gardeners and part-time hobbyists. Every so often, accidents happen. Kids get painted, flower beds get devastated, and fingers get hammered. But it's never serious enough to make us stop.

We're habit-adoring innovators, social hypochondriacs, and fatigued yet frantic. It's not easy to describe Italian vacationers. Sometimes, words are not enough. You need Duane Hanson, the sculptor. One of his most famous works portrays a sturdily built couple who are staring at something in front of them. We don't know where they are, or what they are looking at.

But they might just be in Italy, staring at Ferragosto.

## The garden, seclusion in bloom

From Is Arenas, we went down to Sardinia's Cabras marshlands, where the waters are calmer and less briny. Then we went up toward Narbolia to arrive here at Milis, on the northern edge of the Campidano flatlands. The heights of Montiferru watch over seventeen hundred residents. The green is dazzling after the yellow of the countryside. Black and white, trachyte and sandstone, clad the walls of the churches. The ocher wall of Palazzo Boyl in the village square is a hint of Piedmont in Sardinia. Balzac and D'Annunzio passed through Milis. To do what, I don't know.

It was the Camaldolese monastic community that exploited the waters of the two rivers to grow crops in the *vega*, a Spanish word for a low-lying fertile plain. Eight centuries later, the locals are still tending the island's only citrus groves. In Sardinia, they say that when the first astronaut stepped onto the moon he found a guy from Milis selling oranges.

This place is called S'Ortu de is Paras, which means "the friars' garden." It once actually belonged to friars, but a local family owns it now. The impossibly beautiful gate, which is Pisan Romanesque, marks a boundary. A new territory begins here. It's *verde privato*, a private green space, which is more than just a color or town planner's jargon: it's a psychological definition. If an Englishman's home is his castle, an Italian's garden is his Eden, a place of privilege and temptation. There are no serpents, but there are neighbors.

The Italian garden is an inaccessible place, the quintessence of private property and personal gratification. The modern garden is the secular descendant of the monastic *hortus conclusus,* an enclosed space far from the complications of the outside world, and a source of obsessions and consolations. Do you want proof? Few Italians willingly show you their gardens; they're more likely to take you around their houses. In the Anglosphere, a garden is emblematic of socializing. Radio broadcasts, magazines, conversations, and advice make gardening in Great Britain one way of communicating with others while you're sober (later on, there's the pub). An American garden is a focus of hospitality. Its carefully clipped lawn, on either side of the driveway, is a form of welcome, and the yard at the back is set aside for the pagan rite of the barbecue. We Italians admire this, but we steer well away from imitating you. Our gardens stay shut. Inside our heads, and in fact.

Every spring, small ferocious gardeners behind wire fences and walls get ready to correct the faults of nature, which is sadly lacking in discipline. Some buy books to identify leaves that have yet to bud. Some sow seeds with vigor while spying on next door's efforts, and some return from the Garden Center—English names are all the rage in Italy's suburbia—with RoboCop-style boots, gloves, masks, and other items so fearsome the walnut trees pretend to be dahlias.

The amateur gardener is aggressive because he (or she) is irritable. He is irritable because he doesn't know what to do. And he doesn't know what to do because he is on his own. There's a proverb where I live that tells you when the gardening season begins: *Töte le bròche a Pasqua, le ga bèa la so frasca* (Every branch at Easter already has its buds). This year, things went differently. Until a few days ago, our gardens resembled the economy: they were bare and troubled. Things are better now, at least for the gardens. We're still waiting for the economy to recover, but meanwhile frantic garden owners fuss about at the back of their homes with watering cans and pruning shears. It's best not to upset them. They might take things out on their pets or their violets, which are obviously not to blame.

 *  *  *

It wasn't always like that. Italian gardens used to be places of shared experiments and joyous exhibitions. Think of the "architectural garden" theorized by Leon Battista Alberti during the Renaissance. It was an audacious attempt to control nature by trimming hedges, polling trees, adding statues, creating perspectives, and erecting fountains and bowers. We exported the style very successfully to countries as far apart as France and Russia. The climate may not have been so mild up there, nor the sky so blue, but the importers were full of enthusiasm.

However, it was too carefully ordered a concept. We soon started filling our gardens with monsters and mazes, which more accurately represented what was going on in our minds. Some went even further. Abandoning the architectural model, they opted for a natural or landscape garden, which is less formal and more in tune with our national psychology. Theorized in Britain in the late eighteenth century, the natural garden became popular in Italy during the nineteenth, partly for political and literary reasons, since it was viewed as liberal. With its sweeping lawns, tall trees, bushes, and serried ranks of hydrangeas in the shadow of a wall, the natural garden required little looking after and lots of imagination. How could we fail to like it?

There was a third way, in the shape of the romantic garden, a space that aspired to create a landscape, not fit into one. Plants, trees, and flowering shrubs brightened brief strolls along artificial paths. Gardeners were asked to re-create Arcadia in miniature for Italy's extended aristocracy, which then invited its friends to do battle with horseflies and mosquitoes. But the costs of upkeep and the temptations of selling the land for building have left their mark. Over the past thirty years, the gardens of Italy's stately homes have been cut back and closed in. Tenant farmers have bought out the owners, the middle classes have moved in, and not all of them had romantic inclinations. Trees suspected of keeping out the light have been cut down. Untidy branches have been ruthlessly savaged by amateur pruners, incapable of distinguishing between the legitimate aspirations of a poplar and the ominous incursions of an oak.

The Italian garden has become an oasis of utilitarianism. The dream has been cleaned up, and the private fantasy is available in a range of versions, of which the most extreme and interesting are the vegetable garden, the apartment-building green space, and what we might call the "surveyor's hillock."

* * *

If you want to find out how hardworking the Italians are, look behind the homes in Sardinia, under the electricity pylons in Milan, or around major-highway intersections. You'll find plots that are as carefully groomed as a doll's tresses. Vegetable gardens exist in other countries. In some they're a necessity, in others a hobby. In Italy, they are a stubborn reminder of the feudal economy, providing an illusion of self-sufficiency, a consolation in retirement, and a protest at a country with too many mountains and bridges.

The vegetable garden is a place where social mechanisms are endlessly reproduced. There's solidarity ("I'll lend you my shovel"), suspicion ("Why has she got more water than I?"), competition ("My radishes are redder than yours"), envy ("Your chicory sprouts earlier than mine"), distrust ("I'll keep the key to the padlock"), and pride ("This is my kingdom"). I've known *ortisti* (vegetable garden-

ers) who polish their tomatoes, install complicated irrigation systems, and tile one corner of the plot. Then they gaze upon their
handiwork, and see that it is good. I'm sure the monks of Milis had
the same blissful expression when they contemplated their oranges
glistening in the Campidano sun, lovelier and deeper in color than
the oranges of the monastery next door.

* * *

Another example of the *hortus conclusus* is the apartment-building
garden. In the 1960s, the phenomenon was a new one, and authority was on the defensive. Apartment-building gardens were places
of adventure that left more than one generation with marvelous
memories. Nowadays, they are all wire netting, railings, orders, pro-
hibitions, impositions, and suspicions.

Residents have to adhere to rules like the ones below, drawn up
by a sadistic resident and imposed in the poisonous atmosphere of
apartment-building meetings:

1) Entry is prohibited to nonresidents.
2) Residents are prohibited from playing all ball games.
3) It is forbidden to walk on green areas.
4) Irritating noises and disturbances will not be tolerated.
5) All games of whatever kind are prohibited before 9 a.m.,
   from 2 p.m. to 4:30 p.m., and after 8 p.m. to ensure that residents enjoy peace and quiet.
6) Families of residents shall be held liable for any damage.
7) The administrator's judgment on the appropriate application
   of the above rules shall be final.

They're going about it in the wrong way in apartment blocks.
All they need to do is stick these verses from sixteenth-century poet

Torquato Tasso's *Jerusalem Delivered* on the window of the concierge's cubbyhole:

> The palace great is builded rich and round,
> And in the centre of the inmost hold
> There lies a garden sweet, on fertile ground,
> Fairer than that where grew the trees of gold:
> The cunning sprites had buildings reared around
> With doors and entries false a thousandfold,
> A labyrinth they made that fortress brave,
> Like Daedal's prison, or Porsenna's grave.

This is the description (translated by Edward Fairfax) of the garden of the sorceress Armida, from which the knight Rinaldo escapes so that the liberation of the Holy City can continue. Jerusalem may have come through, but Italy's apartment-building gardens are still waiting for deliverance.

*  *  *

The third type of *hortus conclusus* is the kind around detached one- or two-family homes. You'll see thousands of them as you travel round Italy. The garden is small, square, and well looked after. Vegetal evidence of a middle-class lifestyle, it inspires admiration and a fond smile.

There are low hedges and conventional bushes that have a duty to identify themselves as they grow. Garden gnomes defy the winters and the housebreakers. The owner struggles to grow an English lawn without English rainfall, risking Italian failure.

The topography is typical: the house is on a little hill, and the garden slopes down. Many non-Italians have no idea why this is so.

They've read about the Alps, the Pre-Alps, the Apennines, and the hill country, but those boils on the flatlands are mentioned nowhere in the guidebooks.

The explanation is simple. The hillocks are artificial—created, according to urban legend, by a surveyor, although architects, builders, and owners must share responsibility for them. They have multiple functions, creating space for the garage, making it easier to monitor the territory, and offering the home to the admiring gaze of passersby and the envy of neighbors. What's more, the "surveyor's hillock" is also therapy, because it enables the homeowner to feel like a miniature lord of the manor. The peasants have gone, replaced by garden gnomes.

I wonder if there are any here in the Sardinian port of Olbia, doing sentry duty on the road to the ferries.

# Day Nine: In Crema

## The barber, the newsstand, and the town as lifebelt

Every foreigner's tale of Italy includes—inevitably, immutably—a polite waiter, a friendly tradesman, and a cheerful next-door neighbor. It's a gallery of pleasant people and a litany of names so melodious that non-Italians call out to us even when they have nothing to say: "Giorgio!" "Giovanni!" "Giuseppe!"

I don't question the euphony of the vowels, or the impact of the smiles, but be careful. We Italians aren't insincere, we're ancient, like the Chinese and the Jews. Our courtesy is heartfelt, because we honestly intend to lubricate a social relationship. Our willingness to help is sincere; it's one way of making up for catching you off guard. *Simpatia* gratifies and simplifies; confrontation complicates. We worked that one out centuries ago, and behave accordingly.

Take this barber in the Po Valley town where I was born, Crema.

He works in a narrow street named after a military engineer, full of people walking to the market and cars that shouldn't be there. The barber's name is Gigi, a name that reassures your inner tourist. He knows Italian heads inside and out. Gigi is a professional of the scissors, and of public relations. He talks about politics, soccer, and women. If a woman were to walk in, he'd be able to talk about men and the terrible things they do to their gray hair, for example. Gigi keeps up to date. The radio is always on, and he reads the *Corriere della Sera* and *Gazzetta dello Sport* newspapers. Friends and acquaintances stick their heads in to say hello. It could be a pensioner passing the time of day, or a youngster who wants to eye Greta, the good-looking, Juventus-supporting shampooer.

This twenty-first-century version is not so different from a barbershop in the twelfth century, when Crema, sitting on her marshes and enclosed by her walls, was getting ready to defy the German emperor. A barbershop is still a place for conversations and consolations, a shelter, and a source of information. Obviously, nine centuries ago there wouldn't have been a calendar with a naked lady opposite the shampoo chair. But you noticed that, and you're not Italian.

• • •

Gigi Bianchessi, barber and psychologist, knows nothing of Italo Calvino. To the best of my knowledge, Calvino never met Gigi, yet he did write that all towns have corners of happiness if you know what to look for. In Italy, you have to multiply the corners after recognizing them. Our unsinkable nation is the sum of thousands of places like this that make up hundreds of towns like Crema.

A thousand years of complicated history have produced a mechanism that is perfect in its simplicity. A town like Crema, which has thirty-three thousand residents and lies twenty-eight miles from Milan, is our third line of defense, after the home and the piazza. It's a ring that protects and keeps watch. The ring is ancient, and inside it we know what to do; we end up loving it, sometimes too much. Take a look at the bars as we pass. They are social clubs, and treasure troves of wasted talent. Small-town Italy has a soporific effect. You risk nodding off at twenty and waking up at fifty.

Crema was founded by the Lombards, destroyed by the Germans, and loved by the Venetians, whom it loved back. It admires Bergamo, is suspicious of Cremona, and attracted to Milan. It's a halfway town, the anything-but-mundane aspiration of the average Italian. Two-thirds of my compatriots, it seems, would like to live in a place like Crema. They don't, of course. They turn up here on Sundays, look around, sample the sweet tortelli pasta, and then rejoin the nose-to-tail traffic on the highway home.

A town like Crema doesn't only look attractive to Italians fed up with traffic and suburbia. Non-Italians like it, too. You understand instinctively that it offers the right mix of unpredictability and reassurance. In the 1960s, Luigi Barzini explained Italy's attractions for the rest of the world, and its peaceful invasion by tourists, like this: "The art of living, this disreputable art developed by the Italians to defeat regimentation, is now becoming an invaluable guide for survival for many people."

This is still true, even though tourism has found many other destinations. Everyday life in a small Italian town is an ideal to which peoples more organized than we are aspire. We like our halfway Italy—not too big, and not too small—and have committed to it. A friendly store in our street makes up for bad news on the television. That's why Italy comes out ahead of countries like the United States, France, or Germany in quality-of-life tables. Handcrafted consolations are equal in value to postindustrial organization. Of course, they don't show up in the gross domestic product, but they take pride of place in our personal statements of account.

* * *

Everybody in Italy feels important, and quite rightly demands attention. We know the pleasures of conversation, and savor the tang of personal observations. Comments on a new dress are welcome in Italy; elsewhere, they would arouse suspicion. Italian families defend mealtimes, and the younger generation is discovering the less crucial ritual of the apéritif. We've even managed to transform into a ceremony that most fleeting of habits: drinking an espresso while standing at a bar.

In a town like Crema, we go further. We save time on journeys and lines only to waste it in the piazza or a store. We find time to cycle to school with our children as we struggle with the dog's leash. We've got time for Stefano the philosophical picture-framer, and Paolo the political coffee-roaster who keeps *Libero* and *La Provincia* newspapers on his counter in the hope that someone will read them and say something.

At the end of this street is the covered market, where, on Tuesdays, Thursdays, and Saturdays, the residents of Crema become country folk again. They look, they handle, they haggle, and they ask for explanations. The market is a very functional structure—it's used as a parking lot except on market days—and it's so ugly it's interesting. That bank was once a theater, but it was a café before it became a bank. That building used to be the pawnshop. Today it's split up into apartments. Anyone wanting to write a social history of Italy should certainly study refurbishments.

Take this kiosk. A few years ago, it was the stronghold of one of Italy's monopolies, the sale of newspapers. Today you can buy a paper in some bars, and the newsstand has rediscovered its vocation as a bazaar, a place that sells inexpensive consolations and forgivable temptations. Look at what it sells, apart from papers. There are comic books, fans, toy soldiers, bags, soap bubbles, felt pens, rag dolls, video games, balloons, diaries, notebooks, spinning tops, pottery, DVDs, CDs, decals, scale models, lipsticks, videocassettes, necklaces, pencils, electric toothbrushes, watches, soft toys, watercolor paints, recipe books, handbags, scarves, maps, thongs, folding hats, and disreputable T-shirts.

The back of the newsstand was where the Semi-Undressed Signorina lived until she moved to the TV screen. She was the queen of the sexy comic book, the reading matter of choice for precocious youngsters and childish grown-ups. The newsstand is the shrine where the Deferent Italian comes in pilgrimage to purchase magazines that describe the lives of D-list celebs, Italy's televisual has-beens or never-weres, and former glamour queens pondering meditation or plastic surgery. Lorenzo the news vendor observes and forgives on Crema's behalf, as he watches the traffic coming down Via Ponte Furio with the anxiety of an Inter Milan fan at the start of the soccer season.

● ● ●

Now you will understand why so many Italians say they are dissatisfied with Italy but could not live anywhere else, or miss it dreadfully if they do. Now you know why the provinces are a resource for those who know the difference between the little things and the trivial ones. The world is getting more complicated, so it's nice to have some of your life tools at hand.

In a small town, we don't just want a congenial barber and a well-stocked newsstand. We want professionally made coffee and a proper pizza. We want a couple of streets to stroll down, an avenue to jog along, a pool to swim in, and a cinema for a bit of entertainment. We want a functioning courthouse, a reassuring hospital, a consoling church, and an unintimidating cemetery. We want a new university and an old theater house. We want soccer fields, and city councilors we can pester in the bar. We want to see the mountains beyond the grade crossing when the weather's good and the air is clear. We want footsteps on cobbled streets in the night, yellow lights to tinge the mist, and bell towers we can recognize from a distance. We want doctors and lawyers who can translate abstract concepts into our dialect—my father can—and people with a kind word and a smile for everyone. My mother was like that, and many remember her for it.

We want all these things, and in Crema we have them. That's why I came back to live in the town where I was born, and that's why you're here with me today.

**The monument. And yet it moves**

TO

GIUSEPPE GARIBALDI

THE PEOPLE OF CREMA

MDCCCLXXXV

Look at Garibaldi, with his hat in his hand and two cheeky pigeons on his head. White marble against a blue sky, one of modern Italy's makers watches over a country that is changing, as well as the one that has not the slightest intention of doing so.

New kids emerge from the schools, a Singhalese couple select ice creams, pensioners wait for lunchtime outside the bars, beautiful cars scout for parking spaces among the ugly flower-holders, the

Church of San Benedetto stands guard, and the shops stage their own versions of the human comedy. No one looks up to the statue of the man who one day got angry with his overenthusiastic admirers and shouted: "Romans! Be serious!" One hundred thirty years have passed since that day in 1875, during the general's first visit to the new capital of Italy, but the invitation remains valid. Not just for the Romans, of course.

In Italy, there's a lack of seriousness in public that becomes a question of trustworthiness in private. It's odd that Garibaldi should be commemorated in Italian in a two-word phrase, *alla garibaldina.* This refers to an enterprise begun with carefree audacity, little preparation, and a lot of risks, noted *New York Times* correspondent Paul Hofmann, author of *That Fine Italian Hand* (1990). It's an admirable description of many aspects of Italian life: examinations, holidays, investigations, sports, and even a couple of wars. The statue also proves that our monuments are of more use to visitors than they are to locals. Ask the monuments a few questions. You'll find out a lot of things, including some we don't like to talk about.

For example, they show that everyone in Italy has an eventful life. Statues are no exception. Many have been removed, some have been shifted, others adjusted and stripped of their fascist, monarchical, or imperial emblems. Unlike the fathers of America, who are revered by all, Garibaldi himself has had problems. He was one of the instigators of the unity of Italy, which is still far from complete. One hundred forty-four years after unification, northern Italy and southern Italy still glower at each other and recriminate. But they're like those elderly couples that you can't imagine ever parting—they wouldn't know whom to argue with.

Italy's monuments show something else. Our mistakes continue to disturb us. The Germans have metabolized Nazism, the French have put Vichy to one side, the British have erased some of their colonial history, and the Americans have digested Vietnam. In fact, that's one reason they got mixed up in Iraq. We Italians continue to argue over the fascism we had, the communism we nearly had, the terrorism we tasted, and the corruption we tolerated.

Our digestive process is extremely slow, and induces chronic headaches. The historians may be happy to have something to study, as will the newspapers, which can recycle 1945's editorials today, but the impact on the country is dramatic. While we argue over the past, someone else is grabbing the future.

• • •

Always read the inscriptions. All over Italy, not just in Crema, they speak a language that is different from ordinary speech. This one's on a monument in Piazzale delle Rimembranze, although of course in conversation no one says *rimembranze* (remembrance). Everyone says *ricordi,* or "memories."

BEHOLDEN, CREMA
RAISES UP TO THE INFINITE
THE VOTIVE COLUMN
THAT CONSECRATES TO GLORY
THE NAMES OF HER SONS
WHO GAVE THEIR LIVES FOR THE GRANDEUR
OF THE FATHERLAND.

The memorial is sober, the gratitude heartfelt, and the sentiment sincere. But the Italian is rhetorical. This applies to today's speeches, as well as yesterday's inscriptions.

In public speaking, people say *lustro* (five-year period) and not *cinque anni* (five years). They say *volto* (countenance), not *faccia* (face), and *ventre* (stomach), not *pancia* (tummy). All it takes is a microphone, and the speaker *presenta omaggi* (presents offerings) instead of making gifts. Many people begin letters to shady-dealing university teachers with *Chiarissimo* (Most Illustrious), and everyone signs off with a *Voglia gradire i più distinti saluti* (Please accept most distinguished greetings). It's not clear who is supposed to distinguish the greetings, but the writer feels better for proffering them. I've even seen *Mentre saluto tutti e ciascuno, colgo volentieri l'occasione per confermarmi con sensi di distinta stima* (In greeting each and every one, I am pleased to take this opportunity to reaffirm my sentiments of distinguished esteem). This is the Mount Everest of formality. The air is socially rarefied. Dizziness ensues.

I remember the prime minister describing the negotiations for the liberation of the Italian hostages in Iraq. He didn't say, "We're continuing to talk." Instead, he opined, *"Abbiamo un'interlocuzione continuativa"* ("We have an ongoing interlocution"). The psychological reason for this is the same one that prompts Mr. Berlusconi to use the interjection *Mi consenta* (Permit me). It's a fundamental lack of verbal security that runs through Italian society like a current, from the prime minister's office to the projects in the cities. Language is used as an insurance policy. Or, rather, it's a best suit to wear for photographs, and then put back in the closet.

Our speech is littered with signals indicating prudence. "Where I come from," someone from the Veneto told me, "lots of people start sentences with *Con rispetto parlando* [Respectfully speaking]. When you ask them their name and surname, people in Venice or Padua may reply, *Mi saria Tonon Giovanni* . . . [I would be Giovanni Tonon], with the subtext 'but I could be someone else, if necessary.' " The universal Italian greeting *ciao* derives from *schiao* (pronounced "skia-oh"). In the Venetian dialect, it means "slave," or "your servant." People start out humble, and see how they get on.

Historical explanations have been offered for all this. "The character of the Italians," wrote Giuseppe Prezzolini, "has been formed by two thousand years of Roman law, by the outlines and sharp shadows of mountains, by psychological distinctions and contracts with the court of confession, by political transactions during the quarrels of the communes, by adroitness in setting secret forces against secret forces under absolute rule, by tacit contempt beneath formal obsequiousness to the lord, and by internal freedoms won at the steep price of political subjection." This has led to widespread diffidence. Perhaps we could call it a caution that sparkles in language like a shard of glass in the sand.

In Italy, a certain degree of verbosity, as we were saying on the train to Florence, is adjudged agreeable, and even desirable. For many, it is the hallmark of consequence. Simplicity risks passing for superficiality, and a light touch can be taken for lack of authority. Hence our passion for abstract nouns, our last refuge in lassitude. When you hear an Italian talking about *legalità*, you can be sure he's thinking about doing something unlawful. At the very least, he intends to justify it.

We find the same problem in Italian literature, which aspires to the sublime. If it doesn't quite get there, which is often the case, it slithers into the banal. There is a drawn-out narrative procedure that consoles the teller and reassures the reader. Sometimes it reassures the reader to sleep. The average American novelist will write, "She went to the window, and said . . ." An Italian writer will dedicate a page to the complex psychological process that prompted the character first to go to the window, and then to open her mouth.

In private, we talk quickly and understand one another instantly. In public, we think in a sort of embroidery, expressing ourselves in arabesques. Speaking abstrusely is, for many, a source of pride. It denotes membership of a caste, possession of a skill, and protracted study. It doesn't matter if the listener or the reader understands nothing. In millions of Italians, there exists—sorry, there resists—an astonishing acceptance of obscurity from authority of any kind, be it political, judicial, administrative, medical, or academic. Alessandro Manzoni, author of the classic *The Betrothed,* an excellent novel on Italy's working class, gave us Azzeccagarbugli, a scheming, pettifogging lawyer who glories in the obscurity of his speech. Ennio Flaiano, an expert on the Italian middle class, wrote the impeccably titled epigram "Tutto da Rifare" ("Everything Needs to Be Redone"). It goes:

*Sale sul palco Sua Eccellenza.*
*Esalta i valori della Resistenza.*
*S'inchina a Sua Eminenza.*

Onto the platform comes His Excellency.
Exalting the values of the Resistance.
Bowing to His Eminence.

When? In 1959. Just the other day, in Italy.

＊ ＊ ＊

Memorials in Italy don't just speak through anachronistic inscriptions, astonishing psychological repressions, or predictable poses. Unfortunately, they also speak through neglect.

If you like, I'll take you to see a memorial to sailors that for years was left dirty and waterless, although it's got some grass now, which is better than nothing. There's a memorial to the artillery which last saw fresh flowers on November 4, the anniversary of victory in the First World War. And there's one to a general born in the town that the town can't wait to tear down to expand the adjacent parking lot.

It's not hostility, or even superficiality. It's distraction on the part of a nation that is lively and horizontally oriented, and rarely focuses its attention beyond the very recent past.

But Italy is disconcerting even in its defects. Just as you are about to write the country off as shallow, it reveals unsuspected depths. And when you look into the depths, the surface becomes a mirror. Anything might be going on down there, and you wouldn't know about it.

Take the Tricolore, the national flag. You don't see it much, compared with other countries. Once, this Tricolore aversion concealed a sort of embarrassment, because the national flag was looked on as a symbol for fascist sympathizers. It also masked our detachment, disguised as generic respect: insulting the flag is actually a crime that can get you a custodial sentence. Nowadays, our reserve is only reserve.

We like the Tricolore flag, but don't fly it much. It raises our spirits, but we don't raise our eyes to look for it. The Italian flag excites us, especially after a sports victory, but we don't know how to play with it, the way Americans do with their Old Glory boxers and bikinis.

Yet most of the Italians in Italy, and all of the ones who live abroad, are sincerely fond of the old red, white, and green. They may not remember that the colors come in the order green, white, and red. They may not know the words of the national anthem (the start of the second verse, "For centuries we have been trampled and derided," is confidential). But they've realized that the concept of *patria* (fatherland) is neither selfish nor belligerent.

*Patria* is a mosaic with lots of different tiles. There are family memories and collective fantasies, piazzas, cemeteries, trains, ferries, road signs, musical vowel sounds, the taste of wine, the names of streets, operatic arias, songwriters' songs, perfumes on the breeze, nuances of the light, fields, backs of shops, tollbooths, castles, clothes, newspapers, bad television, good ceremonies, genuine heroes and presumed ones, necklines, and schools.

That's right, schools. That's where we learned a lot of things. Of course, we don't admit this, or even realize we did.

### School, the workshop where shared memories are made

It stands between a park we like to think of as Swiss and the railway station with a faintly Balkan air. It's near a former Korean car-dealer that is now an American-style bar, opposite an Irish pub that's been converted into a club with a half-Polish, half-English name. It's an Italian *liceo,* or high school, and you should pay it a visit.

In 1653, the General Council of the city of Crema wrote, to promote the foundation of the public school that would later become the Alessandro Racchetti Liceo Classico: "The spirits of this city languish without sustenance, while the children deprived of teachers have no one who will nurture in them that thirst for learning which God shall have set in the breasts of men in vain . . ."

Since then, things have improved. The teachers arrived, spirits are sustained, and our children's thirst for learning is combined with a joyful lust for life. God, we are certain, approves.

Let's look at the students. We see sturdy youths, pretty girls, thick hair, and casually exposed flesh. Everyone has a cell phone and a

Vespa. Bikes are chained. Brightly colored backpacks abound. The first-year students look like Snow White's dwarfs carrying rocks from the mine.

Note the backpacks with the SOB label. No, it's not what you think. We have plenty of SOBs in Italy, but they're older and don't advertise the fact outside schools. According to the manufacturer, SOB stands for "Save Our Backs." It shows that Italians like to make up English. Merely learning it is too obvious.

Among the teachers there are heroes, villains, geniuses, slackers, enthusiasts, and incompetents, straggling out like exhausted cowboys after a trying session branding steers. They all get paid to the same scale, taking home an average of thirteen hundred euros a month. For the slackers it's too much, and it's too little for the heroes.

Educating six million students from elementary through high school, and a further two million at university, soaks up 4.5 percent of our gross domestic product. We are one of Europe's least generous nations in this respect, along with Great Britain, Germany, and Spain. Italian teachers suffer from new poverty, old complexes, chronic loss of voice, and low self-esteem. Once upon a time, social prestige was part of the deal. Today families have endless demands and very little gratitude. Teachers are looked on as domestic help, with the added advantage that they don't clutter up the house.

This *liceo* was built in 1962, and conserves that period's enthusiastic ugliness. But many school buildings are former convents, barracks, hospitals, stately homes, or former something-elses. They weren't built to be schools. Foreign visitors think this shows a certain style and aplomb, but the Italians who have to work and study in them aren't so sure. The end result is inappropriate spaces, dark corners, and awkward laboratories, perhaps L-, N-, S-, or U-shaped.

Refurbishing buildings for schools has produced a whole new alphabet. You might find sinks in the classrooms, narrow doors, curious passageways, vertical stairs, or soaring ceilings, which means the room is never warm in winter. Surroundings good enough for a small number of orderly nuns do not meet the needs of three hundred energetic teenagers.

As you go in, you'll see the notice board with its faded gray, apparently identical notices. Many concern meetings already held, trips that have been made, and long-expired deadlines. There's a special sadness in the paperwork of an Italian school, and the corridor is an extension of institutional bureaucracy. The only thing that disturbs it is the presence of the students.

Every school is a laboratory and living proof of certain national characteristics. There's the repetitiveness of the garage-red flooring, the government-issue blue doors, the ministerial-pastel cupboards, the gray umbrella stands, and the sea-green desks. There's tradition in the crucifix and loudspeaker in every classroom, symbols of two kinds of authority. There's routine in the bell whose ringing, unchanged for generations, marks the acoustic frontier between two worlds. There's diffidence in the padlocked closets and the books defended by triple locks, or three officials with only one key. There's involuntary solemnity in the gargantuan snack and beverage machines waiting patiently for custom. There's privilege in the gardens and playing fields used as parking lots by faculty. And there's laziness in the way some principals set up magnificent multimedia rooms and then keep the students from using them. Finally, there's a very Italian paradox in schools that are empty in the afternoons, when the students would appreciate somewhere to hang out or study, and full on Saturday mornings, when they'd much rather be at home.

*  *  *

You will now have realized that education is where old meets new, like two seas stirring curious currents. Italian schools have cost some ministers their jobs, and put up or connived with others, yet the schools survive. They have been promised endless reforms, and actually tried to implement some. In fact, school is a perfect thumbnail sketch of the way we are. It is an example of brilliant imperfection, with peaks of excellence and abysses of inefficiency. But school has achieved one thing. It has held the nation together.

The rituals of school, even the silliest ones, continue to mark the passage of the generations. The names and the rules have changed. Elementary classes have three teachers, not one, who give assessments, not marks. There are class and school councils. The legendary janitors are now "ATA (administrative, technical, and auxiliary) personnel," and the September remedial exams have been replaced by "educational debts." But everything else is still the same.

The low teacher-desks, reflecting authority's loss of status, are still there. The chair backs still splinter in the same way in the same places. Cleaning board erasers still gets you covered in chalk. Coat stands still have an irrelevant hat hook that students hang their coats on. The hook is broken, but forty years of ministerial inspections have failed to spot this.

The most memorable of school rituals is the *maturità*, the school-leaving examination. The future nostalgia of Racchetti students for their *liceo* will be proportional to their grumbling over the next few days. I took the exam thirty years ago, in the crackly heat of 1975. I remember the shock of finding the same heat in Cesare Pavese's novels, and in some of the poems of Giosuè Carducci, whom I suddenly thought I understood. The exam was held behind those windows. I recall the sun hitting my face when I emerged, and the feeling that things were possible.

These are memories that can be shared by a father and a son, or a mother in Crema and a child in Crotone. That's why they're so precious. Nations are like animals: each one reproduces in its own way. We're not British. We have an embarrassed, discontinuous history. Nor are we like Americans. For the time being, our Second of June "Feast of the Republic" can't compete with the Fourth of July. We're not French, either. We're too sardonic to say the word "grandeur" without a smile. Ours is a bonsai nationalism born in school corridors like this one. It shuffles between the desks, steps shyly through the schoolbooks, slides through the identical class registers, and emerges in a party dressed up as an ordeal, the *maturità*. From then on, our patriotism survives on private means and memories.

I know parents who enrolled their children at excellent foreign elementary schools in Italy, and then moved them at fourteen to a classical or scientific *liceo*. They realized that only there do you find the curious glue that, despite everything, binds the nation. Any government that cut back the role of public schooling would lose more than an educational format. It would lose the last training camp for our national consciousness, and we'd be in trouble.

A few days ago, I bumped into a British friend who was in Italy on business. He was inconsolable. A prestigious school, Westminster, had turned down his thirteen-year-old son, after offering him a provisional place. Americans will move to another neighborhood or town to get their children into elementary schools that aren't as good as the ones in Crema. Or spend thousands of dollars every year after subjecting their children to nerve-shattering entrance exams (it's the parents' nerves that shatter; the kids manage). In Italy, selection is postponed, good schools are virtually free, and they teach students how to get along together. There's no metal detector outside the Racchetti, and no one misses it.

Three hundred fifty-two years after the General Council of the city of Crema expressed its wishes, we are admiring a harmonious leavetaking from school. Look at the students as they celebrate the year's end. The office worker's son is hitting on the businessman's daughter, and the doctor's girl is wandering off with the plumber's boy. It's not socialism. It's a social achievement, and we should be proud of it.

# Day Ten: From Crema to Malpensa, by Way of San Siro

Before you make any judgments about Italian churches, you ought
to take a look at a restaurant. That's right, a restaurant. This one's
called the Ambasciata and it's in the Po Valley, near Mantua. It's one
of the best restaurants in Italy, decked out in red brocade, gold vest-
ments, and chalices. Candles provide light, the music of Bach fills
the air, and the room is dominated by a jovial chef as plump as an
abbot. The Ambasciata is a gastronomic monument to the Counter-
Reformation, a concentrate of temptation and bliss that, uncoinci-
dentally, Federico Fellini loved.

Pay a visit and you will see why Italy is a land where frontiers become fuzzy. Restaurants emulate churches, and many churches elicit sensations. They are the product of smells, colors, sounds, flavors, art, kitsch, objects, and overshadowings. As I said in Siena, you need five senses, and a dash of insight, to understand the Catholic faith. The brain will follow if it wants to.

That's why many foreigners don't bother trying to understand an Italian church, and start talking about the Church in Italy. They think too much, and feel too little. They forget that the Catholic faith does not tolerate passion and joy, it demands them.

You can see that in this small church dedicated to Saint Anthony the Abbot, the protector of farmyard animals. Cast your eye around. Note the combination of sincere devotion and vague superstition. There are admirable frescoes and banal paintings, ten saints, twenty offertory boxes, a corner for those in a hurry, a space for souls in purgatory, and an altar for those who want a child. Is it naïve? Perhaps. But this religion mixes it with life, and consoles. In the seventeenth century, people came in to pray for protection from the plague. Today they come to rest and reflect.

This is Crema's *duomo*, the cathedral church. The townspeople started it in 1284 and finished it in 1341, after the previous edifice had been razed to the ground by the usual German emperor. The style is Lombard Gothic, and the lines are clean, inside and out. The brick-work *facciata a vento*—the main façade, soaring above the level of the nave—is stunningly scenic. Look at the clouds passing behind that mullioned window. The architect who put it there was a genius.

People go into the dark and come out into the sun. Many pause in front of the wooden crucifix, which has been listening to all comers for centuries. Some use the cathedral as a shortcut to get to the other side of the square. No one is scandalized. Who said that a place of worship couldn't be part of the family? We have seen more than four weddings and a funeral in here, and they weren't movies.

Every Sunday, the nave and aisles are the setting for various religious functions and society's little set pieces. There are masses for the pious at seven in the morning, for children at ten, the distracted at midday, and for those coming back late from a weekend away at seven in the evening. There are worshippers who never say the responses, as if they didn't want to disturb the celebrant. There are good singers, and those who really shouldn't even try. Some people always sit in the same pew, at the same mass, at the same time, and get upset if someone else is sitting in their seat.

Many non-Italians come, watch, and fail to understand. Yet it's not difficult. Look at the color of the stone in the columns. It's a shade that America will never be able to copy, no matter how it tries. It has taken seven centuries to produce this imperfection, which echoes the equally fascinating imperfection in our heads.

•  •  •

Let's put it this way. Why did vast crowds throng Saint Peter's Square to say farewell to John Paul II, and then to greet Benedict XVI, when Italy's churches are often empty? Enthusiasm for the Pope stands in stark contrast to the difficulties faced by many parishes, which on Sundays look like meetings of the Gray Hair Guild. The youngest worshippers are pushing forty, and have probably accompanied a daughter to the children's mass. The heaving hordes in Rome look light-years away from the tepid commitment of many Catholics. Nine Italians in ten say they are believers, but attendance at weekly mass is falling off. One in three went in 1985; today it's one in four.

It makes you want to ask, "Hey! Where are you on Sundays, you who got as emotional over the Pope's death as young deacons, and were holding forth like elderly theologians? Where are you when the kids take communion, when the youngsters are being confirmed, or when the Scouts are celebrating mass? Why don't you send your child to the parish recreation center you used to go to? Are you the same people who gape at afternoon TV and dream of appearing on the shows?"

Those concerned might choose not to respond, or they might say that you can love the Pope without going to church. I object. John Paul II had rock-star quality, as they say in America, but he refused to give an inch on some things. For him, Sunday mass wasn't an option. It was a duty. Right-wing political chancers laud the John Paul II who defended life, and at the same time laud war. Their left-wing equivalents approve a pope who was hard on capitalism, while also approving abortion. But the people who flocked to Rome for his funeral were more coherent. If they don't go to church on Sunday, there has to be a reason.

Many outside Italy have an explanation. Italians are likable hypocrites. Frenchman Jean-Noël Schifano, the author of *Désir d'Italie*, said some time ago, "Religion is just froth. Useful froth, because it gives you rules to break. Transgression for you is gratification. And I understand you. That's great. Carry on like that." I'd like to tell him that I wish it were that simple.

It is true that the Church-imposed categorical imperative, to be observed, ignored, or circumvented, has been replaced by individual morality, but religion still means something, and Catholics today are no worse than they were yesterday. Many have consciously chosen a faith that was once handed down mechanically from one generation to the next. That choice does them credit. Some have formed groups, and some groups have turned into lobbies. This does them less credit, but it's easy to explain. Many people in Italy seek warmth, a protector, and someone who can relieve the frustration of doubt. Religious lobbies are heating systems, insurance policies, and heavy-duty tranquilizers for a prudent, pharmaceutically aware people.

So why the split personality? Why the enthusiasm in Saint Peter's Square, and the indifference in church? It could be, as we've seen, that a fine gesture comes easier to us than good behavior. It's certainly because the death of John Paul II, the Pope who left his mark on our adult lives, unleashed a storm of emotion. Like, and to a greater extent than, other Western nations, Italy feigns cynicism, but is getting increasingly emotional. We saw this in the reactions to 9/11 in 2001, the Nassiriya massacre in 2003, and the tsunami in 2004. In the case of John Paul II, other factors also come into play, such as mystery, familiarity, affection, esteem, emulation, and emotional impact.

With some exceptions, Sunday mass fails to strike the same chords, the ones that prompted the early Christians to descend joyously into the catacombs, and inspire African Americans to sing gospel music at the top of their lungs. It has to be admitted that believers should not bear all the blame. More than a few priests contribute to the decline with unconvincing services, and boring, recycled sermons. When the collection plate goes round, the offering should be proportionate to the giver's appreciation. A rough-and-ready parish poll like that might encourage corrective action.

Actually, it's not such a bad idea. The father-figure Pope whom we saluted with such emotion would probably have endorsed it. John Paul II would have collected more than anyone, raking in a fortune every time he spoke.

•  •  •

Italians are a moral people, but our morality, like our law, has to be tailored to fit. We have an à la carte approach. Everyone selects what he or she wants, according to conscience and convenience. Religion is still fundamental, but the menu is long, and the dishes varied.

The starter is a classic. It's our distrust of authority, cultivated over centuries of foreign domination. As a starter, it's predictable but indigestible, for it prompts us to justify antisocial behavior. Almost anywhere else in the Western world, a professional who declared a quarter of his real income would be embarrassed. In Italy, he feels like a silent avenger.

Our first course is equally famous. I refer to the attachment to family that makes some Italians think they can use any hook (or crook) when relatives' interests are at stake. Years ago, an American sociologist called this "amoral familism," the tendency to behave well inside the family, and to pursue private advantage outside it. The idea is alluring, but simplistic. As we have seen, the family is a high-powered car, but you can drive it. You don't have to let yourself be run over.

We've also already mentioned our entrée, the Italian pride in intelligence, which prompts us to prefer pointless complication. Rules are dull; breaking them attracts us. But we forget two things. In human society, the discipline of the many is as important as the genius of the individual. And to mistake cunning for genius is to equate Michelangelo with an interior decorator.

We should explain one of the other items on the menu, our penchant for transcendence. What do Italy's transcendents say? They say that there is a superior good, for which it is legitimate to sacrifice something. Honesty, in many cases. Objectivity, in others. The odd principle here and there. For example, what moves our religious transcendents? The idea that you can join forces with, and adopt the methods of, the worst to promote your own ideal. How does the political transcendent behave? He announces that if the ends are worthy the means don't count. This is the poor man's Machiavelli that has caused endless trouble, from fascism to communism, socialism, terrorism, Berlusconism, and pacifism.

The next item on the menu is important, but little known. It's the intimacy that slides into connivance. Italy is a land of people who like being together. We socialize easily, and use that ability to establish relationships. This is a good thing, until relationships form between controllers and the controlled. That's when the problems start. That's why the Parmalat scandal and other great Italian disasters came about.

Nor is the side dish widely known. It's our antipathy for authority, which surfaced in the late 1960s and grafted itself onto our traditional individualism. In church, school, university, work, families, and couples, top-down rules irritate. We all want to decide for ourselves. But Italy missed out on the Protestant Reformation, and for many people, deciding on their own is hard work.

Now we've come to the sweet, and it's bitter. We expect to be forgiven. The concept of punishment is not very Italian. Amnesty, even more than absolution, is our banner. Explanations? One, perhaps. Since we don't trust authority's motives or honesty, we have an emergency exit. Possible indulgence is our antidote to probable injustice, our detergent for a dirty conscience.

We saw this in the 1990s, during the Clean Hands campaign. Judicial investigations revealed an endemic corruption that half the country knew about and the other half suspected. After the initial indignation, many Italians started to worry. What were these magistrates doing, demanding that all laws should actually be obeyed? Some, like Silvio Berlusconi, included psychological denial in their election programs. By sidestepping confessions and both his and our repentance, Mr. Berlusconi earned first applause, and then votes. Looking back, it couldn't have gone any other way.

## The stadium, notes on social gastroenterology

I don't think there are any scholars of the Italian weekend. For a start, they'd have to work on Sunday, and not everyone wants to. But I get the feeling that our weekend is changing, for the better, after risking the worst.

The weekend, with or without a hyphen, is a British invention: the Oxford English Dictionary traces it back to the mid-seventeenth century. We have imported it along with other Anglo-Saxon habits, such as democracy, soccer, and striped shirts. The word *week-end* (with a hyphen) appears in A. Panzini's *Dizionario moderno*, published in 1905, and in 1919 *La Stampa's* Paris correspondent wrote about "what the British call *week-end*, when, in general, you don't do anything."

The mass phenomenon appeared later on, in conjunction with two other events, the shorter working week, and private transport for the masses, in the latter half of the 1950s. Workers at the Fiat factories did not leave the poorer parts of Turin to spend the weekend at expensive resorts like Sestriere, but some piled the kids into a Seicento subcompact and took them for a trip to the seaside. In 1964, the word *weekendista* (weekender) appeared for the first time in the *Corriere della Sera*. The trend had started. In these cases, lexical monstrosities like *weekendista* tell you we are comfortable with a new concept. Two decades later, Italians had learned how to *faxare* (to send a fax); nowadays, *messaggiamo* (we text) with our cell phones.

What has happened in forty years? If I had to put it in a nutshell, I'd say that the weekend started out as a tentative discovery but has turned into brazen masochism. There has been a mutation of the initial idea, which was that the weekend was time off, when it was possible to go on a trip or twiddle your thumbs, depending on your mood and the weather. Millions of Italians now think they have to give their lives meaning between Friday afternoon and Sunday evening. This has disturbing consequences, especially for city-dwellers. Compulsory weekenders now face nose-to-tail traffic to get away, and more to get back, with two days of frantic activity in between.

Some of these weekenders are now the stuff of legend. A Milan-based yachtsman will drive hundreds of kilometers to Liguria to justify the price he paid for his boat. A Po Valley skier rents a chalet in Switzerland and then commutes. Once, her ancestors made a similar trip, but they didn't have a ski rack on the roof of the car. There are also Lombard-country lovers who don't sit around counting poplar trees in the sunset. They head for the *autostrada*, and then shut themselves up in a cottage in Tuscany. They'll spend the next two days surrounded by euphoric English couples who invite them in for drinks, and ask them what they think of Giorgione, who turns out to be a Renaissance artist and not the local plumber in Colle Val d'Elsa.

●　●　●

Sunday has suffered the consequences of being squeezed into the weekend. There was even talk of abolishing it, at the European Union's behest. The discussion that followed was peppered with accusations, recriminations, selfishness, and fundamentalism. Spiritual, ritual, traditional, psychological, sports-related, work-related, and school-related arguments were all brought to bear in support of opposing conclusions. The Church defended the Lord's Day, thinking about mass. Hypermarkets stood up for seventh-day shoppers, thinking about their sales figures. But what are people who are neither clerics nor retailers to think?

The first conclusion is that the Italian Sunday has changed. Like the night, it has become elastic. Thirty-one Italians out of a hundred work shifts—in transport, hospitals, bars, and newspapers. Among university graduates, the figure is forty-eight out of a hundred. Thirty-three percent of Italians go shopping with other people. Many supermarkets are open, and lots of other shops have applied to do the same—obviously, not the ones we need, like bakeries or vegetable shops, but the ones that need us, like clothing stores. The question really ought to be: Do Italians want to hang on to what is left of Sunday? Do we still want to keep our chaotic, part-time, exhausting, imperfect, discretionary Italian Sunday?

The answer is yes. It's important to us because it's part of our way of life. The weekend is a foreign invention, but Sunday is ours, an opportunity to do something special for a nation that is suspicious of change but horrified by routine. We have mass, mass travel, exhibitions, eating out, bicycles, *bambini*, brimming car trunks, and boisterous dance floors. We have Sunday drives and car-free Sundays. On Sundays, we stretch our legs, spring-clean our homes. The new festive fever needs only a setting and an excuse. Usually, it finds both.

Giving up Sunday would be like abolishing Ferragosto. There's no reason to. Many Italians say that after six days at work they need a little peace and quiet. Then they find themselves snarled up on the road out of town, elbowing their way down the main street, or unable to stretch out on a packed beach. That's when they realize they enjoy collective celebrations more than they fear crowds. This is Italy's sweat-stained patriotism. So let's hold on to it. It's better than nothing.

\* ● ●

On Sunday, there's also soccer. Actually, there's less of it than there used to be on Sunday. Today there are also championship matches on Saturday, and during the week. But the habit survives, and many remain faithful. Some take part in the afternoon ritual, others attend the *posticipo*, which in modern Italian no longer means "I put off." It now refers to the Sunday-evening game. Both are enthralling spectacles, live or on television. But you cannot claim to know Italians until you've seen them at work inside a soccer stadium.

I set foot in Milan's Stadio San Siro for the first time when I was eight, and I remember the impression made by the vertical terraces, the heads that looked as if they were painted on the sky, the green pitch, the white goals, the black-and-blue banners, and the colors of the other side (Lazio, sky blue and white). I brought my son here when he was the same age, to see a disastrous defeat by AC Milan, the other local team. It was the start of his love affair with Inter. He realized at once that the team was a gaggle of engagingly unpredictable madcaps, and thoroughly deserved unquestioning passion.

Sniff the air. A stadium has its own aromas: the wind from the parking lot, acrylic, mini-salami, beer, and a soupçon of suspense. But one way or another, the match will produce a result, in a country where almost everything is postponed. A stadium is a nudist camp for emotions. Verdicts are drastic, angers violent, euphoria excessive, and forgiveness instant. Modern Milan is much like ancient Rome, with soccer players at San Siro and gladiators in the Colosseum. Today there aren't any lions, but there are TV cameras.

The stadium is a laboratory. The numbered seats serve to conduct an ancient experiment in which our nitpicking culture of quibbles melds with enthusiastic flouting of the rules. If a ticket says Sector T, Row 5, Seat 011, its holder will expect to sit there, making the occupant move somewhere else, even if the stadium is half empty. A few minutes ago, he may have parked on the median strip, but the lack of consistency does not perturb him. A numbered seat is a right, and heaven help anyone who tries to take it away. Parking responsibly is a duty, which means it is negotiable.

An Italian stadium, like an Italian road, is a place to exercise discretionality. As I said, the rules exist, but everyone interprets them in his or her own way. A general rule is viewed as boring, as well as an imposition. Defying or protesting it is one way of making it interesting. In a stadium, even criminal offenses, from insults to physical threats, are transformed into sociological excesses. There are aggressive types, designated victims, loud protests, and dubious absolutions. Some people have even tried to play down the awful scene in the Champions League derby match with AC Milan, which was suspended, on television live to the entire world, after a deluge of rockets and bottles. Incidents like these make soccer stadiums unsuitable for children, who love them dearly for the same reason.

An Italian stadium is proof that even when Italians are together in large numbers they remain distinct from one another. The polo grounds described by Don DeLillo at the start of *Underworld* are a powerful fresco of American life (all the "people formed by language and climate and popular songs and breakfast food and the jokes they tell and the cars they drive"). In contrast, the terraces at San Siro are a huge collection of Italian miniatures. Eighty thousand solitudes, each with its own anxieties, expectations, memories, disappointments, psychosomatic disorders, and plans for the evening.

An Italian stadium is a melting pot of irrationalities made all the more intriguing because it is operated by a rational people. Anxieties, even those of Inter Milan fans, are unjustified. Every team faces more disappointments than final victories. Yet fans continue to

go, putting up with endless hardships unknown in British or German stadiums. Getting to the match is an effort. Parking is complicated. The stairs are tiring to climb, and endless on the way down.
Getting out is arduous. There's always a car with emergency lights
flashing that is blocking the traffic to let some big cheese leave.

An Italian stadium is a pyramid. At the top are the clubs, owned
by a generous industrialist, an ambitious builder, a dodgy financial
whiz-kid, or a successful dealer in soccer players. All of them know
that a soccer club will bring them protection, friends, prestige, and
notoriety, as long as the money lasts and their nerves can take it. In
the middle is the bourgeoisie of the upper deck, and the middle
class of the lower deck, subdivided by length of service, repute, experience, vocal power, and arrogance. Beneath is the plebeian aristocracy of the terraces. Here, too, there are all kinds, and everyone
speaks to everyone else. A crowd in a stadium knows that soccer offers what our culture denies us, and politics only promises: partici-
pation in a nationwide conversation. You've been to Italy when you
know the result of the Juventus game, not before.

A stadium is a maze of privileges, discretionary powers, prece-
dences, codes, and hierarchies. The number of ever-popular executive boxes is on the rise. They offer exclusiveness for the masses,
a concept that we Italians refuse to consider a contradiction in
terms. There are Sky Boxes and Executive Stands, names that are
so provincial they're romantic. You can sense the longed-for eleva-
tions of power achieved and rewards enjoyed. In reality, they are
tiny apartments that can hold thirty people clutching a sandwich.

In its own way, every soccer stadium in Italy is a paradise. Every
steward feels like Saint Peter, which is why they work for nothing.
The role ensures that weekly dose of self-importance without which
no Italian can survive. There are colors (red stand, orange stand,

green ring, blue zone), membership cards, season tickets, certificates, badges, stamps, bracelets with passes, passes without bracelets, acquaintances who let you in anyway, and uniformed young women who smile with seraphic, impartial incompetence.

So you see an Italian soccer stadium is a summary of what we are, by mistake or by good fortune. It's a space suspended somewhere between tribalism and the modern world, a place where tens of thousands of separate people come to share something, a fantasy world, an album of memories, the preparation for a disappointment, the expectation of joy, a selfless love, and the remains of their Sunday.

## The horizon. In other words, give us back Columbus

Ten days ago, you had a few not very clear ideas. Now you have lots, but they're confused, which is a good sign. If Italy doesn't leave you bewildered, it means it has conned you.

Your trip is nearly over. We'll be at Malpensa Airport in an hour. There's not much traffic, because on Sunday evenings people are coming back to Milan from the lakes, and we're heading in the opposite direction. Look at the guy admiring himself in the rearview mirror as he waits to pay the toll. I wonder where he's going, and what's on his mind under that sleazy cap.

I like seeing countries from behind the wheel. In America, the road is a category of the mind. It's not in Italy, or not yet. Departures and arrivals come too close together. There are too many breaks, too many tolls, too many snarl-ups, and too many bends. The heart doesn't have time to attune to the beat. That's why there's no Italian Bruce Springsteen. We've got the poetry, but not the kilometers.

On a June evening, you get an insight into the Po Valley from an automobile. It's a fascinating bowl where all sorts of things have been bubbling away for two thousand years. There used to be barns; now there are industrial buildings. There used to be barbarians; there still are, but nowadays they're manufactured locally. The final battles are fought out on the roads. There are deaths, as pointless as any others.

The landscape, too, has changed. The mulberries, flax, rye, and hemp have gone. There's much less wheat, but more corn and soybeans. Rice is still widely grown in the west. Compared with a century ago, the flatlands are drier, and look almost American. There's less marshland, less cultivated land, fewer trees, and fewer colors. Green dominates in a way that almost always astonishes those who arrive over the Alps, whether they are invaders or holidaymakers. From a satellite, some 95 percent of Italy's surface area—thirty million hectares, or almost seventy-five million acres, half of it cultivated—looks green. It's a monochromatic richness in which we see many shades. In contrast, the Italian horizon has had a much more colorful past. It's been cut up by roads and power lines. It's been fragmented by farmers. It's been broken up by industrial buildings. It's been taken over by town planners and traders.

The flatlands are no longer cadenced by poplar trees and bell towers. Towns and villages fray at the edges into a straggle of gas stations, car dealers, shopping malls, and fast-food outlets. Farmhouses are declarations of good intentions in the middle of the fields. They survive, but frequently they are empty. People live elsewhere. Over the past half-century, the population of Italy has risen by nine million, but the number of available bedrooms has shot up from thirty-five million to one hundred twenty-one million, not counting unauthorized accommodations. Like the farmhouses, many homes are empty. They wait for weekend visits, and a bit of excitement during the summer holidays.

Take this Lombard horizon home with you. It's an unusual souvenir. Leading up to it are patchworks of fields, networks of ditches, and tributaries homing in on the Po. In fall, it's hidden by the fog, which round here is a moral atmosphere, as well as a meteorological one. It doesn't bother us. We've got plenty of experience, good fog lamps, damp hearts, and romantically rheumatic joints.

*  *  *

We worry about another horizon, one that's hidden by Italy's uncertainty, not the Po Valley fog. For some time, new things have frightened us, and it's not easy to see why. Our poor, authoritarian country got back on its feet after the war, and in sixty years became democratic, wealthy, and modern. It shouldn't be afraid of the future. But it is. We are a young democracy with incipient senescence. If there were endocrinologists for nations, we'd be making an appointment.

The symptoms are obvious. We've talked about them over the past few days. Our birthrate is low, investment is in short supply, our infrastructure is aging, research is struggling, and some of our worst habits persist. That's one of the reasons so many young people leave the south for the north, and Italy for elsewhere.

What's more, consumption focuses on instant gratification. Hi-tech fripperies abound. Advertising offers consolation, not progress. One Italian in two now seems to be a cook or a wine expert. The other one's a taster. Fashion repeats itself and reassures. Television is a cathode-ray-tube copy of a village fair, complete with showman, hunky guys, and a well-endowed girl looking after the shooting gallery. Some, irritated or content, call it a "Berlusconized" society. Others, with amused condescension, say Italy is "Brazilianized" in its obsession with hedonism and body care.

Perhaps there is an analogy closer to home. Early-twenty-first-century Italy brings to mind Venice at the end of the eighteenth. The partying went on and on. Carnival continued in endless episodes. "In this city," said one traveler of the day, "all is spectacle, entertainment, and sensual delight." In his *Storia d'Italia* (*History of Italy*), Indro Montanelli wrote, "Pleasures compensate for oppression, and help to bear it. And Venice's dominant caste was an excellent dispenser and director of pleasures."

Then as now, the horizon is limited to the next diversion. Fashions delude the naïve, telling them they are edgy. Pleasures help us to forget a ruling class that changes but never for the better, a stagnant economy, and an unworkable legal system. Civil actions that drag on for an average of seven years are an incitement to offend, and a slap in the face for the honest. People know this, but are powerless. Politicians could do something, but appear not to understand.

Silvio Berlusconi promised he would be the captain who would turn the ship around, but instead he concentrated on making his own cabin comfortable and ran aground. Before trusting him, most Italians believed in Mussolini, socialism, America, the magistracy, or Europe. They're all incarnations of the same myth, a Zorro who rides up to win on our behalf. But Zorro is for kids. We need Christopher Columbus. We need someone to point out the horizon, chart a route, encourage the crew, and show us how to keep a steady hand on the tiller.

Unhappily, we have no Columbus, and sail on without a chart. In fact, we're a long way from the safe haven of a quiet, democratic society where people talk about how public services work and school vacations. Planning infrastructures, supporting research, thinking about education, simplifying trade, securing energy, rationalizing services, promoting competition, and reforming the professions are challenging projects. Why not just have a good time? It's so much easier.

⁕ ⁕ ⁕

Our sun is setting in installments. It's festive and flamboyant, but it's still a sunset. Many non-Italians are surprised that such a dazzling nation should seem so tired and cynical. Unlike Luigi Barzini, I don't think that foreigners come here because they wish "to take a holiday from their moral duties and evade their national virtues." I think that you have understood what we merely suspect: this unpredictable Italy is still a special place, and it is sad to watch it struggle.

"It is difficult to define with precision the happy, insubstantial atmosphere that makes up Italian life, a mixture of good humor, wit, and live and let live, which does not preclude depth of thinking, audacious skepticism, a certain sensual passion that is also romantic, full of understanding for human nature and tolerance for vices and virtues." The words are those of Giuseppe Prezzolini, a passionate, embittered Italian writer and intellectual. When he came back from New York in the 1960s, he went to live just over the Italian border, in Switzerland. His was love from a safe distance, but love it remained.

It is yet another demonstration that national feeling in Italy exists. It's complicated, angry, buried beneath rhetoric, sarcastic, and camouflaged in cynicism. But it exists, and can even be gracious. It was there in Prezzolini, who fought it; in Barzini, who exported it; and in Montanelli, who concealed it. It's still there in the many Italians who yearn for a better country but no longer seem able to dream the dream. And it's there in the guy at the gas station cleaning our windshield. He's smiling, though it doesn't say he has to in his employment agreement.

The feeling may be tradition, or habit, or merely a break between one argument and the next. There's probably a bit of regret mixed in there, too. We know that in the end our virtues are inimitable, but our defects could be corrected. All it takes is the will to correct them. All it takes is the belief that the Italian mind is a jewel, not an alibi.

EPILOGUE

# A Letter from America

Dear Beppe,

We're back home in the States, and the effects of our trip are
starting to sink in. My daughter doesn't dare ask for a cappuccino
after ten in the morning—you said it was immoral and probably
illegal—and my wife has started to question the American practice
of mandatory tips. This will probably get us thrown out of our favorite Italian restaurant, and we'll have to pay you another visit.

Let me tell you right away that next time we intend to see
Venice. I'm sure you'll trash all our fantasies about the lagoon, just
as you shattered our American dream of Tuscany. We'll take that
risk.

We understand now that your Italia is not our Italy. Do you
know something? We're not sorry about that. The Italia you

showed us is just as fascinating and less predictable. We like the country we saw with you. We like its coffee shops, beaches, trains, piazzas, homes, and churches. There really is a *dolce vita* in Italy, but it's not something out of a film or a vacation brochure. The Italians who, like you, contest the tyranny of the picturesque are right. Italy is too seductive to fit onto a picture postcard.

This is just a thank-you letter. Cappuccino-related psychological terrorism apart, you helped us to understand that people can listen to and learn a country like a song, if they have a good ear and a little patience. Even when the country leaves you bewildered. Something you said stuck in our mind. "Italy is the only workshop in the world that can turn out both Botticellis and Berlusconis." Well, you could say something similar about the United States. We have produced George Washington and George Bush. We in America also know how to alternate genius and gaucherie.

Still, it's true. You're never really ready for the Italian jungle. No other nation is as good at difficult things, like cooking, aesthetics, and family relationships, or—and please don't be offended—as lackadaisical over the easy ones, like sticking to the rules, organization, or administration. I remember what you told us at the airport before we left. Italy's good qualities are the inimitable product of centuries of history. Its failings are the annoying consequence of civic idleness. That's why you added that Italy is the kind of place that can have you fuming and then purring in the space of a hundred meters, or the course of ten minutes.

Americans visiting the land of the *bella figura* are more generous. We purr a lot and fume only occasionally. You could say we're euphoric when we arrive, become bewildered, and then start to get the hang of the place. For example, here are some of the things we learned on our ten-day trip with you.

1. You can trust the restaurateur's advice and professional skills during your meal, less so what he puts on the check.
2. You can have a glass of wine with your lunch and no one will think you're an alcoholic.
3. You shouldn't put more than ten ice cubes in your Coke or else you might have to pay for them.
4. Never leave more than ten inches in front of you in a line, or five yards on the highway; otherwise, some joker will slip in ahead of you.
5. Roadside billboards are dangerous. It's just not possible to observe Italian undress and Italian traffic at the same time.
6. Pedestrian crossings are there for decoration only.
7. In Italy, motorists, small children, priests, and good-looking women do whatever they want to.
8. Don't be surprised if private gardens are untidy. Failing to cut the grass is not a criminal offense in Italy.
9. In Italy, the first floor is where the second floor should be.
10. In Italy, you've got to keep repeating your given name. Italians forget what it is, but it doesn't mean they don't like you.
11. Some Italians will fall over themselves to convince you that you're their all-time best friend for this week. If you believe them, that's your fault.
12. None of the preceding rules is any use. If Italians realize that foreigners know them, they just make up some new rules.

I think I know what you're thinking. On our ten-day trip, you said some things that were more important. I know, and I haven't forgotten. Let me jot down a couple of shorter lists. There are four things in the Italian mind that confuse Americans, and four more that we love. The confusing ones begin with an "i"; the others start with the letter "g."

INTELLIGENCE You explained, and we agreed, that intelligence is overused to the point of exasperation in Italy. You don't just want to decide "what kind of red" a stoplight is. If it lasts a second or two longer than expected, people think it's out of order and go through it anyway. There are towns in New England where they'd have to dig the driver out in March if the stoplight broke down in December. No one would jump a red light. There's no danger of that in Italy, and it's not just a matter of climate.

INTUITION It's true that intuition in Italy is almost uncanny. Sometimes it serves as a substitute for what we Americans call "homework." The upshot is, if I may say so, that Italy is often left behind by less talented nations, simply because they're more disciplined.

INTENTIONS Often these are good, which is to your credit. But good intentions in Italy are not always accompanied by good groundwork. The predilection for improvisation—another "i"—is, I think, self-evident. Obviously, people take pride in resolving complicated situations with a stroke of genius, but wouldn't it be better not to get into those situations, perhaps by applying a touch of boring foresight?

INTIMACY   In that Milan nightspot—the girls were stunning, by the way—you explained that Italians can tune in to other people's wavelength with spectacular speed. There is no apparent effort, and no alcohol involved, but you find things to talk about, flash little smiles of complicity, and identify shared interests. This is admirable, but sometimes you don't know when to stop. Relationships become more important than rules, job-selection processes, or lists of qualified applicants. Foreigners in Italy on vacation spot this and chuckle. But non-Italians who come on business get annoyed. They don't understand the rules of the game, and sometimes refuse to play.

Those are the four criticisms. Now here are four qualities that we Americans envy.

GENIUS   This is not just the genius of Leonardo, or the less spectacular but still-delightful version of Italians who invent recipes, clothes, and objects d'art (in America, chairs and shoes have to be comfortable; Italians prefer sexy). The Italian genius can be seen in everyday behavior. Take the recent law that bans smoking in public places. Let's be honest, no one expected the law to be obeyed. But it was, and obeying it wasn't regarded as an act of contrition, as it would have been in other countries. Quite the reverse. You manage to enjoy yourselves. Did you think I didn't notice the smokers schmoozing outside the restaurants? One young man told me he had started smoking because he met so many girls that way. Tell me who else could manage to turn a crisis into a party?

GUSTO  We're talking about gusto in the English sense of keen enjoyment and in the Italian meaning of good taste. Everyday life in Italy has plenty of both in its beautiful locations, welcoming homes, good food, excellent wine, friendly people, and reassuring, multifunctional families. You can't complain. You explained that in small towns this formula is narcotic. You risk nodding off at twenty and waking up at fifty. It has to be said that there are more dangerous drugs, and worse places to take them.

GUTS  I'm not talking about the business ethics of the Sopranos, or the way taxi drivers behave. We were ready for that ("Frequent travelers to Italy are familiar with the symptoms of Taxi Terror: feverish prayer, piercing screams, loose bowels, and cardiac arrest," from the phrase book *Wicked Italian*). I'm talking about the way you Italians tackle life's complications. The determination with which you have seduced invaders, metabolized governments, and overcome economic difficulties is laudable. You may be a bunch of "fifty-eight million unique cases," as you say, but feeling unique is good for your self-respect. There's more irritation than desperation around in Italy, so good for you.

GENEROSITY  There's an underlying generosity in Italy that we in America are losing. Foreigners are not objects of suspicion; they are an amusing diversion. I remember one incident in Tuscany. You weren't with us that afternoon. We asked the first gas station for directions in our broken Italian. We weren't able to make ourselves understood until a biker turned up. He had a rugged face, a bit like Joe Perry from Aerosmith. Then another biker arrived. Then two more. They didn't understand us. We didn't understand them. We looked at one another like beings from different planets. Then the Tuscan Joe Perry worked it out. We wanted to go back to Siena, avoiding the main road. So the giant got onto his bike and signaled us to follow him along narrow roads and across incomprehensible intersections. His three friends tagged along behind. I imagine we were the first American family to enter Siena with an escort of four bikers. Fra Angelico met Hunter Thompson, and the results were exciting. This gratuitous, inquisitive generosity is also evident in the way almost all Italians treat immigrants. It could be the absence of colonial hangovers, but the atmosphere in your country is different from that in France or Britain. If you don't build any ghettoes, you'll be able to show the way forward. Italian generosity is also evident in other attitudes that you may not notice anymore. We do. There's the absence of chauvinism, the self-criticism, and the almost childlike inquisitiveness toward others. A foreigner is never an outsider in Italy. That's why many of us keep coming back and find you enthralling. You don't just look at people in Italy; you see them. That's a nice surprise for new arrivals, and it helps us to forget lots of other things. Even your cappuccino fixation.

And by the way, why can't you have one after dinner? Would you please explain, once and for all?

# Acknowledgments

My sincere thanks go to my family, many friends, a few colleagues, and all the good people who keep this country going and pretend that nothing is wrong.

# About the Author

Beppe Severgnini is a columnist for *Corriere della Sera,* Italy's leading newspaper, and was Italy's correspondent for *The Economist* from 1996 to 2003. In addition to *La Bella Figura* (a number-one bestseller in Italy), he is the author of the national bestseller *Ciao, America!* and several other books. He lives in Crema, Italy.